LIFE
WITHOUT
Limits

100
Inspirational
STORIES

KEN TAYLOR

outskirtspress
DENVER, COLORADO

Contents

Introduction...vii
The Underdog 1
Bad Weather.. 4
No Limits.. 6
Unconquered!... 8
Angel of Mercy.. 10
Dreams to Reality 12
The Timid Saint!.. 14
Sight and Insight... 16
Spend Wisely! 18
Miracle on Ice 20
Taking a Trip 22
The Words of a Leader... 26
Problem Solver?... 28
You Decide.. 30
A Friendly Person 32
Failure...A Road to Success! 34
A Date with Destiny 36
The Finishers 38
The Real Story 40
Garages of Destiny 42
Critics Don't Count... 44
211 Degrees 46
Monday, Monday 48
The Race of Life.. 50
There is a Santa Claus.. 52
Life Isn't Fair 54

Don't Ever Give Up! 56
Overnight Success 58
The Hidden Leader 60
A Cut Above 62
The Extra Mile 64
Never Discount an Idea! 66
Writing Your Own Ending 68
The Law of Explosive Growth! 70
Keeping One Foot on First 72
Don't Make New Year's Resolutions 74
Eternal Youth 76
Victim of Circumstance? 78
The Rocket Boys 80
Live Like You Were Dying 82
If I Could See 84
The Greatest Law of the Universe 86
What Life Have You Touched Today? 88
Dangerous Words 90
Mirrors or Windows? 92
Lessons from Geese 94
Taking Poison 96
Adversity Creates Power! 98
Attitude is a Choice 100
How Could I Be So Lucky? 102
Change This, Change Your World 104
How to Motivate Others 106
Making the Best of Life 109
The Buck Stops Here! 111
The Greatest Gift 113
The Greatest Gift 115
Are You Avoiding Difficulties? 117
Compass or Clock? 119
Daily Goals 121
Focus on the Invisible 123

Living Large 125
Overwhelmed? 127
Ripples on the Pond of Life 129
Answer the Call 131
Necessity.. 133
Risk and Reward....................................... 135
9/11 Remembered 137
Your New Year's Recipe 139
Troubles 141
Rainy Days and Mondays 143
Unlimited Power 146
The Power of Fear..................................... 148
Motivation by Example 150
Turning Lemons into Lemonade................ 152
Words and Actions 154
Fear, an Asset... 156
Focus... 158
Keep Playing.. 160
The Three "C's" of Success!...................... 162
Hidden Talents... 164
Oh Say Can You See 166
Timing that Changed History 168
The Blame Meter 170
It's Only a Game...or is it? 172
Good to Great 174
Run to Win!... 176
Fido the Dog 178
Ice Cream Anyone?.................................. 180
Homeless to Harvard................................ 182
Saved! 185
An Unlikely Hero 187
The Last Basket.. 190
Having Vision 192
Little Margy 194

Play Ball! 196
Put Me in Coach! 198
The Import 200
The Unlikely Sharpshooter 202
Gone Fishin' 204
The Race of a Lifetime 206
Thoughts to Live by 209
In a Pickel! 211

Introduction

For the last ten years, I have written a one page motivational article for the many newsletters and publications for which I write. This book is a spinoff of those articles. The positive comments over the years have been overwhelming and in a way they have made me realize the awesome responsibility we all carry with us day in and day out, the ability to touch lives for better or for worse. A single word has the power to crush a dream or inspire greatness. This came to light for me while I was still a high school coach at Orange Park High School in Orange Park, Florida.

I was athlete director at the time as well as head track coach and a classroom teacher. One of my athletes—who graduated two years earlier—drove hundreds of miles for a single purpose, to thank me for saving his life. As we both shed tears he recounted his story of a terrible accident that brought death to his doorstep. That door never opened and he pulled through. After he left my office I sat in silence contemplating the incredible power and influence I had in this young man's life. His story is contained in the pages of this book. From that moment on I became more cognizant of my words and actions. I carried an incredible responsibility as a high school coach. I could destroy dreams and lives, or I could build them. I have spent my life doing the later.

There are different types of articles in this book. Some are stories of athletes who overcame impossible odds, some are young children who inspired others but never made it to adulthood. Many are not stories at all, but ideas and concepts put into words. My hope was to make others think as they read the words and maybe, just maybe, the words would make a difference.

I have found one thing in all my research, there is no shortage of incredible people in this world whom have accomplished great feats. They have overcome impossible odds to accomplish incredible things with no intent to be famous or the next viral YouTube story. They simply wish to survive the monumental obstacle before them. You will read stories of lemonade stands on a summer day, military heroes, oil refineries, suicide, and illness, but each one will leave a lasting impression upon your mind and heart.

If you find the stories inspiring or life changing, send me a testimonial to ken@coachkentaylor.com so I can use it in my next book or if you have an inspirational story please send it to me and I will make a commitment to contact you and if possible include your story in my next book. A portion of every book sale will go to St. Judes Children's Hospital in Memphis, Tennessee. St. Judes is one of those special spots on earth where brave children come to fight for their lives.

We all have a responsibility to give back in this very short life and I hope this book will inspire you. I want to say a special thank you to all the many people who have touched my life, including my high school coaches, Carl Duncan, Ron Crawford and Gene Willis, my college coach Dave Braine, my favorite all time teacher, Brenda Osborne, my business mentor and friend Bill Carroll, my children Rick and Christi Taylor, Josh and Caleb Matthews, and the love of my life, my wonderful wife, Ricki.

Who is Ken Taylor?

Ken is known nationally as "America's Corporate & Personal Coach." He speaks to thousands of people every year and is president of Ken Taylor & Associates, Inc., a training and consulting corporation. He graduated from Orange Park High School in Orange Park, Florida and attended the University of Richmond on a football scholarship.

Ken was a teacher and coach at his alma mater, Orange Park High where he coached three high school All Americans in track and field and seven athletes that went on to play in the NFL. He returned to coaching temporarily when his son reached high school age. The team, Nease High School won a state championship and Ken was fortunate to have coached Tim Tebow, the former University of Florida Heisman Trophy winner and collegiate All American.

Ken's business clients have included General Motors, Chrysler, Ford Motor Company, Mercedes Benz USA, Citi, Wells Fargo and many others.

The Underdog

DESPITE BEING CHOSEN to receive the Golden Helmet Award from the Denver Post as the best high school football player in the state of Colorado, Freddie Steinmark went unnoticed by colleges. His 5'9" 150 pound body just didn't fit the "profile" of what even the smaller colleges wanted. That changed when Coach Darrell Royal of the University of Texas saw film on the diminutive player and decided to take a chance. He sent one of his assistant coaches, Fred Akers to Steinmark's hometown of Wheat Ridge, Colorado. Akers rang the doorbell of the Steinmark residence and thought the young man who answered the door must be Freddie's little brother. The high school athlete was invited on an official visit to the Texas campus. He wore boots with high heels, hoping to look taller on his visit.

Coach Royal meet with the young athlete from Colorado and Freddie was shocked by what the coach told him. "Son, let me tell you something very interesting," Royal said. "I didn't get to the University of Oklahoma until I was 25 years old, because of the war. I was just about your size. I quarterbacked the Oklahoma Sooners to a national championship one year. On defense, I broke the record for interceptions. I don't care how big you are."

That day, Steinmark committed to UT and made a vow to himself that he would start every game. He did not care how high the odds were stacked. When Steinmark arrived for fall practice, sophomore rover Mike Campbell mistook him for a team manager.

"The kid looked like he was 15 years old," Campbell recalled.

That was before Steinmark was issued a uniform and began knocking freshman teammates all over the field. In 1967 freshman football players could not play varsity, but Freddie made his mark on the freshman team by leading in interceptions and completing a 76 yard punt return against Texas A&M.

At the very start of his sophomore year, he replaced the starting safety and fulfilled his dream of making first string for the Longhorns. He was making good grades, attending college with his high school sweetheart, and never missed mass at his church. The season started out slow with a tie and a loss, but after James Street became the starting quarterback in the Texas wishbone offense, they produced eight straight wins, a Cotton Bowl victory over Tennessee, and ranked third in the nation.

The 1969 season began with great promise for the Longhorns and Freddie Steinmark was a preseason All Southwest Conference selection at safety. Over that summer, before the 1969 season, the owner of the dealership where he worked noticed Freddie limping. When he arrived on campus it was evident to the coaches that something was wrong. Despite the limp he performed on the field and Texas breezed through a nine-win season.

The limp got worse during the season and the Texas coaching staff considered benching Steinmark, but after much thought they felt his contribution to the team's 18 game winning streak earned him a second chance. He pulled through and remained the most devastating hitter on the team.

The final game of the season was against Arkansas, with Texas ranked number one in the nation and Arkansas number two. Freddie Steinmark played like a champion with Texas, winning in the last minutes of the game. After the game, one of the players noticed that Freddie was crying, but it was not from being overjoyed, it was from the tremendous pain in his leg. Three days later, he confessed to Coach Royal that he had trouble walking. He was sent to Houston's

M.D. Andersen Hospital for x-rays and they discovered an abnormal growth in his left thighbone. After a biopsy was performed it was confirmed that over an inch of his femur had been devoured by cancer. Emergency surgery was performed to amputate his left leg at the hip.

Within a few days he was up and walking on crutches and vowed that he would be on the sidelines in nineteen days when Texas played Notre Dame in the Cotton Bowl. When he came out of the tunnel at the game he received a standing ovation from the entire stadium. Twelve days later, he walked across the stage on a shiny new prosthetic to receive his letter jacket from Royal. There was not a dry eye among the 6,000 fans at the Austin Municipal Auditorium.

He never gave up, he learned how to drive a car with one leg, water ski, and learned to play golf. He asked his high school sweetheart to marry him and she accepted. The wedding day was never to be, the cancer had spread and in May of 1971 Freddie Steinmark left this world. His funeral in Denver, Colorado is said to be the largest crowd in the history of the state.

When players run through the tunnel before home games at Texas there are two large photographs of Freddie Steinmark. Each player touches a picture and gives the "hook 'em horns" sign as a tribute to a young man they have never met, but who remains an inspiration to this day.

What Freddie Steinmark taught was not about dying with dignity, it was a roadmap on how to live life to the fullest with no excuses and with full effort. Even in the worst of circumstances Freddie Steinmark took full responsibility for how he lived his life. As each day unfolds let it be your best day. That's what Freddie did.

Bad Weather

IT IS OFFICIALLY a record! The most airline flights cancelled in a single day due to bad weather! February 13, 2014 was a day of stress, less than acceptable behavior toward airline personnel, and quite a few family arguments that most likely started out with the statement, "George, do something!" The airlines did not muster up the bad weather to play a joke on customers and, in fact, dread days like "Thursday the 13th."

Let's take a different look at the situation from the school of "the glass is half full." Every life, every business, every family goes through tough times often for reasons that cannot be controlled, like the weather. Energy can be funneled into the "blame game," or the "let's take it out on somebody else" school of thought. Great organizations and great people take these kinds of obstacles in stride. How? It is called "preparation, productivity positive and politeness." Let's look at how these work in combination to turn the worst of situations into success.

A seasoned traveler knows that something will go wrong on every trip and he or she is prepared with work projects, reading material and alternative plans such as the key airline numbers, a phone app that locates nearby hotels and eating places, as well as emergency numbers. This same preparation applies whether you are working on a project or trying to start a business. If you prepare for the obstacles there is no surprise and you are ready for any situation.

Productivity is funneling energy into worthwhile ventures, which don't include screaming at the airline personnel. When obstacles appear your preparation allows you to use your time in an energetic, positive, and productive way. You might complete a work assignment that has been lingering or contact friends to say hello. Productivity is finishing the day far better off than you started.

Remaining positive through tough times is not an easy task, but one thing is certain, you will attract good things into your life when you expect the best rather than complain about what cannot be controlled. People will recognize that you are different and are appreciative of any efforts made on your behalf. Positive energy attracts more positive energy just as negative energy pulls bad things into your life.

Finally, good old fashion courtesy and politeness will put you above the crowd in volatile times and others will acquire your calmness and warm heart. We attract to us what we send out. Treat people with kindness and respect and most of the time you will receive the same emotion from others. Eric Hoffer said, "Rudeness is a weak imitation of strength." Seldom does a rude person win over the crowd. Actually … he alienates them. It is a reflection of the rude person's insecurity. There is great strength in treating people as you would want to be treated.

The next time you face a difficult situation remember the four "Ps" and put them into practice. You will be amazed at the stress that leaves your body and the calmness that enters your life. Pass it on!

No Limits

HE WAS BORN in Madison County Florida, east of Tallahassee. In high school Carl was a three-sport letterman in football, basketball, and track. A starter in all three sports. Watching Carl was an amazing thing, he could dunk a basketball, easily defeat double team blocks in football and was a standout in the high jump, shot put and discus in track and field. None of this seems very amazing; many high school athletes compete in three sports. The thing that sets Carl apart is that he competed in all three sports with only one leg. No, he did not wear a prosthetic leg. He actually competed with one leg. When asked why he did not wear his prosthetic leg, he replied, "it slows me down!"

Carl Joseph had many outstanding performances. In one varsity football game he made eleven tackles, blocked a punt, and intercepted a pass. He went on to play college football at Bethune Cookman College in Daytona Beach, Florida. In college, Joseph became known for his special-teams play. "The impact on all of our kids and on how they perform is something," said Coach Bobby Frazier, Bethune Cookman's head coach. "When it's rough and Carl's in there, we know we can do it. I'd love to see what he'd do with all his limbs."

In 2009 Carl Joseph was inducted into the Florida High School Athletic Hall of Fame for his contribution to high school sports and his inspiration to young athletes.

Carl coached high school football for 15 years and now serves as senior bishop at the Holy Jerusalem Church of God in Tallahassee,

Florida. Health problems have slowed him down physically, but his heart is as big as ever. "I've always said that I never thought of myself as handicapped," he said. "It was never talked about in my household, so I always considered myself an average kid. I always felt I could do with one leg what kids did with two legs."

Most people sell themselves short. Their biggest obstacle is not the opponent, not outside obstacles, but their own way of thinking. Carl never considered himself handicapped and believed in his heart he was as good as anyone. The deep-seeded belief that you will succeed no matter the odds—that you triumph on your own terms—will in the end put you on the victory stand. Thank you, Carl!

Unconquered!

AT THE AGE of 13 he contracted tuberculosis of the bone and at the age of 17 it was necessary to amputate one of his legs below the knee. Despite his disability he rose to become one of England's most prominent literary figures. His friend, Robert Louis Stevenson used the "one-legged" poet to create the fictional character of Long John Silver in his classic novel, "Kidnapped." Stevenson later confessed that he admired his friend's strength of character against adversity and felt compelled to create the image of a one-legged pirate who had the power to lead people.

Illness continued to plague the life of this much-admired literary figure. He was faced with the amputation of his remaining leg until he enlisted the advice of Dr. Joseph Lister and was admitted to the Royal Infirmary of Edinburg for three years. During this time of great pain he wrote some of his very best poems.

The author and publisher married and had a daughter who died at the age of five. Some of his greatest works occurred after her death and he passed away from tuberculosis nine years after his daughter Margaret. This writer, poet, and publisher was Ernest Henley. Perhaps his most quoted and remembered work was the poem "Invictus," which was a testament to how Henley lived his life despite illness, constant pain, and personal loss. The last stanza of the poem is often quoted:

"It matters not how strait the gate,
How charged with punishments the scroll.
I am the master of my fate:

I am the captain of my soul."

Every day we are faced with tough choices. The stresses and troubles of the modern world can seem overwhelming at times and personal loss will be a part of everyone's life. It is not what happens to us, but how we react and grow from the tragedies and obstacles that shape our lives and our souls. Live each day to the fullest and do not allow life to defeat you...be the master of your fate and the captain of your soul.

Angel of Mercy

SHE WAS BORN as Irena Krzyanowska in Poland on February 10, 1914. When she grew up she became a social worker and nurse just in time for the Nazi occupation of Poland. Her married name was Irena Sendler. Employed by the Social Welfare Department, she was allowed to enter the Jewish Ghetto where the Nazis had forced anyone of Jewish decent to live or be sent to the concentration camps. Irena had one duty of which the Nazis were not aware, the rescue of Jewish children by Zagota, the Polish underground movement.

Irena headed a group of women who were allowed into the Jewish Ghetto to aide in outbreaks of various diseases and to inspect the housing. They left with far more than they entered. In all it is estimated that Irena and her group smuggled out over 3,000 Jewish children. She was directly responsible for the rescue of over 400 infants. They were smuggled out in suitcases, toolboxes, even disguised as packages. If they had been discovered it would have meant a very brutal death at the hands of the Nazis.

The children were placed with Polish families, the Warsaw orphanage of the Sisters of the Family of Mary, or Roman Catholic convents such as the Little Sister Servants of the Blessed Virgin Mary Conceived Immaculate at Turkowice and Chotomów. Sendler worked closely with Zofia Kossak-Szczucka, a resistance fighter and writer, and with Matylda Getter, Mother Provincial of the Franciscan Sisters of the Family of Mary. Sendler and her group carefully labeled each child by name and parents name, placed the names in a glass jar and then buried it in a neighbor's yard. Her hope was to reunite the children with their families after the war. Unfortunately, most of the parents died in concentration camps.

In 1943, Sendler was arrested by the Gestapo, severely tortured, and sentenced to death. egota saved her by bribing German guards on the way to her execution. She was listed on public bulletin boards as among those executed. For the remainder of the war, she lived in hiding, but continued her work for the Jewish children.

In 1965, Sendler was recognized by Yad Vashem as one of the Polish Righteous among the Nations. A tree was planted in her honor at the entrance to the Avenue of the Righteous at Yad Vashem. She was also awarded the Commander's Cross by the Israeli Institute. That same year the Polish communist government allow her to travel abroad, to receive the award in Israel. In 2003, Pope John Paul II sent Sendler a personal letter praising her wartime efforts. On October 10, 2003 she received the Order of the White Eagle, Poland's highest civilian decoration, and the Jan Karski Award, "For Courage and Heart", given by the American Center of Polish Culture in Washington, D.C. She was also awarded the Commander's Cross with Star of the Order of Polonia Restituta.

When asked about her efforts her reply was, "I was brought up to believe that a person must be rescued when drowning, regardless of religion and nationality. The term 'hero' irritates me greatly. The opposite is true. I continue to have pangs of conscience that I did so little."

She willingly put her life on the line and yet still felt as if she fell short. True courage can best be defined as the willingness to sacrifice all, even life for the benefit of those who cannot fight for themselves. Today is a great day to give of yourself…pass it on.

Dreams to Reality

WHAT GREAT DREAM would you dare to undertake if you knew you could not fail? If it was 100% guaranteed that your efforts would result in fulfilling your greatest wish, what would you attempt? Too often we read the stories of great achievers, close the pages of the book, and wonder, "How could I ever accomplish my dreams? I'm not like these people; I don't have what it takes." You are right in only one respect; you are not like these achievers because you have not started! Life does not reward dreams that sit idle in the minds of people, life rewards dreams turned into action. Thinking a great thought or dream is like holding the seed of a great oak tree in your hand, but not planting it. You can hope for a mighty oak, but it will not come to pass.

Why do we not attempt the thing that keeps us awake in the midnight hour stir us as we daydream of what could be? It is many things, but most of all fear. Not just fear of failure, but fear of effort, ridicule, and even of ourselves. In the 1800's one of the first motivational books was published by James Allen. One of the most inspiring and thought provoking paragraphs of that book is the following:

"Man is made or unmade by himself. In the armory of thought he fashions the weapons with which he destroys himself. He also fashions the tools with which he builds for himself heavenly mansions of joy, strength, and peace. By the right and true application of thought man ascends to divine perfection. By the abuse and wrong application of thought he descends below the level of the beast and between these two are all the grades of character and man is their maker and their master.

Of all the beautiful truths pertaining to the soul, none is more fruitful of divine promise and confidence than this; man is the master of fate, the molder of character, the maker and shaper of condition, environment, and destiny."

Dust off the dreams within your heart. Believe in your right to glory and start on the path of greatness. An old Chinese proverb states, "The journey of a thousand miles begins with the first step."

Here are a few life suggestions that follow the ideas of James Allen:

- Your thoughts are the guiding light of your life. If you fill your waking moments with positive thoughts it will alter the actions that you take leading to a more fulfilled and prosperous life.

- Repeat positive affirmations stated in the present tense. Never say to yourself, "I will finish a novel" Instead say, "I am a novelist who writes daily.

- "Never let outside influences determine your thoughts or your actions but rather internal influences of positive thinking and creative thoughts.

- Be so passionate about your dreams and desires that you enlist the support of others who will help you reach your dreams. Everyone wants to be a part of something greater than themselves. The more cheerleaders you have, the better!

Today is your day, today starts your first step to your destiny, step with passion!

The Timid Saint!

LATE AT NIGHT some of our most important thoughts come to us. Past memories, unfinished tasks, but most often "what if" or "should have" thoughts dominate our thinking. These are all the things that could have changed the course of our lives. The investment we didn't make, the property we didn't buy, the career we passed over, or the book we never wrote come to us and we wonder what would have happened?

We observe the "great people" in history and we assume they are made differently than the rest of us, that they possess extraordinary talent or intellectual genius and in many cases that is true, but the real story is far more revealing. The fact is they do possess a few traits that are within everyone's grasp. Here is a story that reflects those traits.

Early in life she was so timid and shy that her family worried about her ability to relate to people and forced her into a special school to socialize her. This attempt backfired and the young girl went into deep depression. It was only after her brother was injured and she nursed him back to health that she found her calling, helping others. She went on to become a successful teacher. Moving to Washington D.C. she became one of the first women to be hired for a government position as a clerk in the patent office and paid a man's wages which was unusual for the time. The Civil War changed everything.

The young woman felt compelled to go to the frontlines and tend to wounded soldiers. She had no background as a nurse, but through common sense and a passion to help she attracted other women to the battlefield and initiated practices that were unheard of, such as clean bandages and antiseptic treatment of wounds. She became known by Union soldiers as "the angel of the battlefield." After the Civil War she ran the "Office of Missing Soldiers" and went on to found the American Red Cross. Clara Barton possessed no medical background, was by nature very shy, and yet changed the course of American history. What created her greatness? A few traits that are within each of us and, if nurtured, can create greatness.

- A passion for our true calling in life. Helping others was the one thing that fulfilled Clara Barton and becoming a battle-field nurse was her way of giving back to the American cause.

- Unrelenting determination to succeed. It was recognized quickly that she gave her all for the cause of wounded soldiers working 24 hours a day in some cases to make a difference.

- A focus on the "one thing" that lifts the soul and spirit of each human being. It is different for each of us but when found can lead us to the path of success. Don't confuse the "one thing" with money, fame, or power, it can only be equated to the impact it has on making the lives of others better.

Is there a book inside of you that can inspire others? Is there a local charity where you can make a difference? Is there a talent you possess that can touch lives whether a sense of humor or a need to help? True greatness is not measured in fame or fortune; it is measured in lives touched and the unselfish works that change the world for the better, whether in your family, your community, the nation, or the world. Start today!

Sight and Insight

JAKE WAS BORN a healthy baby. Until he was ten months old. The doctors diagnosed the tiny infant with cancer in his left eye. There was no alternative but to remove it. Jake was a fighter from then on, never using his loss of sight for an excuse not to do his best. He played sports and especially loved the game of football which he participated in until tragedy struck again when he was almost twelve years old, cancer in his right eye. The family was devastated, except for one person. Jake.

Jake Olsen was a diehard University of Southern California football fan and wanted to be able to see a practice before he lost sight in his right eye. Pete Carroll, former head football coach of USC not only invited Jake to practice, he was on the sidelines for an actual game. The team even hoisted Jake on their shoulders after a victory. When the surgery approached the young boy told his mom, "It's time for a new chapter in my life and I'm ready."

Jake missed football and the excitement of games, so he started thinking, "Surely there is a position that I could perform blind?" The answer came to him, long snapper! You don't have to see the holder or kicker, just practice until you get the feel. Jake made the varsity football team at Orange Lutheran High School, perfected his long snapping ability and along the way made a difference. Jake became an inspiration to his team, his school, and the world. ESPN did a special on Jake, he appeared on the Katie Couric Show, and much more. He has co-authored a book, and carries a 4.4 grade point average.

The most amazing thing about Jake is his attitude and his insight. He plans on attending USC and becoming a motivational speaker. Don't bet against him. "I want to be recognized after I leave this Earth as Jake Olson, a man who defined his circumstances instead of letting his circumstances define him."

Tomorrow you will wake up and before you rise you will think about your day. Do you hate getting out of bed? Jake doesn't. Are you stressed over things you can't control? Jake's not. Do you feel handicapped from reaching your dreams? Not Jake! The definition of a successful life is not money or fame, it is taking what gifts you have and making a positive difference in the world. Jake may be blind, but he has incredible vision. The great Helen Keller, deaf and blind at a young age, said, "The most pathetic person in the world is someone who has sight, but no vision."

There is no limit to a person who has made the single decision to see all of the possibilities life offers, to never sell him or herself short, and to believe with both heart and soul that the world holds endless rewards. Thank you, Jake, for showing us that sight is not required to have vision.

Take your vision and put it into action every day of your life and you will never be short on confidence, determination, and miracles! The glorious and unexpected always happen to people who never limit themselves to the endless possibilities of a life lived to the fullest! Carpi Diem! Seize the day!

Spend Wisely!

SUPPOSE EACH DAY $86,400 was deposited into your banking account with one requirement, that you spent every penny on worthwhile things. At the end of the day your account would be wiped clean and any unspent money would be taken out of your account never to be seen again! You would probably focus on making sure you spent every dollar wisely.

The $86,400 is the same amount as the number of seconds in a day. If you think about it, any second you do not spend to its fullest potential is lost forever. One of the biggest factors in success is how you spend your time. Highly successful people all have one trait in common, the effective and efficient use of time. Ben Franklin said, "You may delay, but time will not."

Some people are born with more talent, some with more intelligence or better appearance, but we are all born with one level playing field, time. No one has more time than the rest of the world. The real secret to success is how you use the time. So how can you leverage time to reach the dreams and aspirations of a lifetime?

The first step is to eliminate time wasters. Useless television, people who take your time, and activities that do not add value. Ask yourself a simple question before you take on any activity, "Does this add value to my life and to my dreams and goals?"

Once you eliminate time wasters the second question to ask is, "What adds value and allows me to move toward my dreams?" Make a list and put it in priority order. This very simple list is actually your life plan. Call it your "to do" list of success.

Next separate your plan into major categories. I call them the six "Fs." Faith, Family, Friends, Fitness, Financial, and Fun. Under each category list your goals.

Once you have your goals, list the major actions you can take that will lead to the successful completion of those goals. Here is one of the most important lessons you can learn: Take well planned, focused, and relentless action and miracles begin to happen in your life.

Here is a coaching tip. Put your "F's" on separate 3 X 5 index cards and review them at the start of every day. Choose one action in each area and take action that day. Individuals who waste the 86,400 seconds each day will quickly fall behind you while you will climb to the top.

Here is one additional card you will need, your daily "Start Card." On this card you put the critical things you will do to start each successful day. On my start card I have the following:

- Do 100 pushups and crunches immediately on rising.

- Read one chapter in your Bible each day.

- Repeat all of my affirmations immediately.

This is the shortest card but the most powerful to start your day with positives.

Miracle on Ice

THE YEAR WAS 1960 and the impossible happened. The Soviet Union lost in Olympic hockey to a young group of college hockey players from the USA. Embarrassed by the loss, the Soviets vowed to build a powerhouse that could not be defeated and went on to go 27-1-1 after their Squaw Valley loss. They destroyed their opponents with a 175-44 margin of goals scored. The Russians went on to win four consecutive Olympic Games leading up to the 1980 Games in Lake Placid, New York. They outscored the Americans 28-7 over that same time period.

Prior to the actual competition at the Winter Olympics of 1980 the Soviet hockey team defeated the National Hockey League All Stars 6-0 and embarrassed the US Olympic team 10-3 in an exhibition match in Madison Square Garden immediately prior to the start of the Winter Olympics.

The US team was a group of college players coached by Herb Brooks, head coach at the University of Minnesota. Brooks was a task master and chose players not based purely on talent, but on the best fit for the style of hockey he knew he would have to play against the power-house Soviets. To put the game in perspective, the US team was given little hope of surviving long enough to meet the Russians. The day before the game, Dave Anderson, a reporter for the New York Times, wrote, "Unless the ice melts, or unless the United States team or another team performs a miracle, as did the American squad in 1960, the Russians are expected to easily win the Olympic gold medal for the sixth time in the last seven tournaments." The ice didn't melt, but the Soviets did.

Herb Brooks was a task master who tried to intimidate his players and worked them to exhaustion while teaching them a European style of intense and tactical play, knowing that the Russians would try to intimidate this group of kids. The US had surprised the world by tying Sweden in the opening round. Then came a stunning 7–3 victory over Czechoslovakia, who was a favorite for the silver medal. With its two toughest games in the group phase out of the way, the U.S. team reeled off three more wins, beating Norway 5–1, Romania 7–2, and West Germany 4–2 to go 4–0–1 and advanced to the medal round from its group, along with Sweden.

They faced the Soviet Union in the semi-final game and fell behind early, but went on to win 4-3 over a panic stricken Russian team. The impossible had become possible. A group of college kids defeated the World's best hockey team. The US team went on to beat Sweden to win the Olympic gold but the real victory had already happened. Brooks is credited with a superb coaching job but the real story is one of belief, dedication, and perseverance against impossible odds.

Too often in everyday life we give up against far less odds. So much of life is going into any situation with an attitude of belief and the willingness to give any amount of effort to achieve the task at hand. Anyone with a dream, a desire, and the will to win can achieve greatness; just ask a group of kids with a dream!

Taking a Trip

I LOVE TAKING trips! It is always exciting to see new places and explore the unexpected in life. As much as I love to travel there is one trip I don't like taking, the "guilt trip." This is always a miserable journey whether someone else is asking me to take the journey or I am forcing it on myself. The guilt trip is always filled with anxiety and despair, not to mention stress and depression.

Others try to send you on the guilt trip for a variety of reasons. Most often it is to try and control you or purposely attempt to make you feel bad. For some reason they think it will make them feel better if they can transfer their negative emotion to you. Eleanor Roosevelt once said, "No one can make me feel bad without my permission." In a sense, allowing someone to make you feel guilty is a self-inflicted punishment. You beat yourself up and let the other person control you. Here are a few tips on refusing to take the guilt trip:

- Even if you actually did something wrong admit to yourself that you were wrong and you will make every effort to correct the mistake. If necessary, apologize! A sincere apology is a way to transfer guilt and regain your freedom.

- If the other person refuses to accept your apology, the ball is in his or her court. You can tell yourself that you did the right thing and live guilt-free.

- Make amends. When a store makes a customer service error the best organizations practice something called "symbolic atonement." This means they do something to make up for their mistake in the eyes of the customer. It might be a cheerful refund or a gift certificate for the customer's troubles. Do something for the person you offended, such as an apology card or letter.

The worst guilt trips are the ones we impose on ourselves. Very often these trips are based on a long-term state of mind. Carrying guilt around long-term is like taking poison and waiting for someone else to die. After a while it begins to eat at the very core of well-being. Once again there are steps you can take:

- If the guilt is based on a long ago injustice to someone, it is never too late to correct the situation and often it becomes a more powerful act of redemption when done years later. Maybe you offended a relative or friend years ago and never allowed for forgiveness. Correct it through a conversation or letter coupled with a sincere apology. What's important is not that they accept your apology, but that you sincerely delivered it.

- Often long-term guilt is based on acts of omission rather than commission, something you failed to do. Make a list of commitments you promised to fulfill and then accomplish them one at a time. What is important is progress on a daily or weekly basis.

Guilt may be one of the most destructive forces to the human mind. Why not start today with a new kind of freedom, freedom from guilt. A person with the strength to forgive one's self is free to forgive the others and that is the ultimate freedom.

Yes, But...

Few good things come after, "Yes, but..."

"Yes, I forgot to turn off the stove, but I was busy doing other things!"

"Yes, I did not meet my sales goals this month, but there was a lot going on."

"Yes, she said that's what she wanted me to do, but I didn't think she was serious!"

The "Yes, but..." combination is basically a statement used by people who do not want to be held accountable for their actions. "Yes, but..." is also a way to recognize someone's positive attempt and then immediately discredit the action or act.

"Yes, you told me you loved me, but you didn't say it with meaning!"

"Yes, you finished the report on time, but there were numerous mistakes!"

Using this dangerous combination of words gives the recipient hope and then dashes it on the rocks of life. People who use the words together may be right, but the result is wrong. A "Yes, but..." manager is usually viewed as very negative by his or her direct reports. A spouse who is a "Yes, but..." person drains the other person's emotional bank account with half compliments that are filled with sarcasm. What is the alternative?

How about separating the positive from the negative or in the case of accountability, separate the "Yes" from the excuse. When you compliment a team member or a close relationship, make it from the heart with no strings attached! If you need to correct performance or relate how you feel to someone close to you, do it at another time and make sure your feedback is factually based. Make it, if possible, in questioning form to let the person have the first attempt at correcting his or her own actions or performance. "John, how close are you on your sales goals so far this month?" If John freely admits he is behind, you just look deeper and guide John to his own solution. "John, what do you think has hindered you from reaching your sales goal that is within your control?" This well worded question forces John to admit he could have changed some things to improve.

Combining positive feedback with negative feedback actually has a greater negative impact than only negative feedback! When you gave the person hope that he or she is getting a compliment, it is a big emotional drop to sandwich it with a negative, far more than if the person were expecting only negative. This is a critical skill for all managers to learn and anyone who has close personal relationships that are sometimes tense.

When you first eliminate "Yes, but..." from your vocabulary, expect those around you to be confused at first. "Is this the same John from yesterday?" will be one of many first comments you receive in the beginning until people adjust to the new and more positive you! Once they adjust, you will find them willing to open up more, to seek your advice more often, and even give you more effort in the workplace!

Never underestimate the power of being positive, yet assertive. You will not only attract talented people, you will enjoy the job of a leader, coach, and mentor. Wise men are those who speak little, think much, and never stop giving more than they get! These acts of positive influence will ripple from person to person like the concentric waves upon the pond of life. One day someone may ask, "What type of leader was that person?" The answer will be, "Someone who made a difference in the lives of others." With a little effort, a lot of attitude, and the desire to make a difference in the lives of others, the person they talk about could be you.

The Words of a Leader

THE BEST LEADERS are those who lead by example, but there can be little argument that throughout history, great leaders have been great communicators. Winston Churchill inspired England through its darkest hours. Abraham Lincoln's few and powerful words at Gettysburg inspired a nation and still inspires today. It is not always a powerful speech that most inspires those who follow us, but what we say day in and day out that touches those around us. One mark of a great leader is not only what he or she says, but "how" it is said. Consider this ancient story and how a message's delivery can impact its meaning.

A King once had a dream that he had lost all his teeth. Concerned about the meaning of the dream, he sent for a wizard who was known to interpret dreams and see the future. The wizard listened intently to the King and after some thought, he began his interpretation. "Mighty King, the meaning of your dream is this: all those who are dear to you shall die before you, and you will be left alone!" Furious, the King called for the royal guards and banished the wizard from the kingdom.

Still troubled by the dream, the King sent his knights to search for another wizard who might be able to give a different interpretation of the dream. They found such a wizard and brought him before the King. After hearing the substance of the King's dream, the wizard gave the following interpretation. "O wise and mighty King! You should celebrate with great happiness! You will live long and prosper! In fact, you will outlive all of your relatives! Hail to the King!"

The King was overjoyed and issued a proclamation of celebration throughout the Kingdom! As for the wise wizard he bestowed upon him great riches and a permanent place as the King's chief advisor.

The talent of a great leader is the ability to take any message and turn it into words of encouragement and learning! The next time you are faced with having to deliver bad news or a critical message to an employee, friend, or even family, choose your words carefully. The same message can either inspire or depress. Here are a few communication tips that will help you.

- Before you present any bad news to a group or individual make sure you have explored the potential positive spin offs of the news. Someone's job might be eliminated, but through research you might find an alternative position.

- Be honest in your communication, but at the same time use positive words of encouragement.

- Be willing to confront concerns and objections during your conversation. To avoid or delay them reflects a degree of insincerity and possibly dishonesty. Trust in the leader comes from a direct, positive approach to communicating with others.

Carefully choose your words in any given situation, reflect great empathy, and be solution oriented and the world will acknowledge your greatness.

Problem Solver?

SO MANY PEOPLE pride themselves on being a problem solver. A customer or fellow employee has a problem and he or she is quick to try and solve the problem. To the extreme, this person cannot exist unless he or she has a problem to solve. If this person is a manager, his or her entire day is spent putting out fires and doing a great disservice to other team members. A manager who spends the day solving other people's problems is ineffective at best, and at worst, prevents people from growing and becoming more valuable employees!

The great managers and leaders are "problem preventers." What are the steps in being a proactive leader who eliminates problems and focuses on getting to the next level?

- When a team member brings you a problem, rather than immediately telling this person what to do, ask for an opinion on what he or she thinks.

- If the team member's idea or solution is correct, congratulate them for an excellent decision! Let this person solve the problem and be a hero!

- If the team member's idea or solution is wrong, ask the person about the thought process that brought him or her to that conclusion. Once you have done this, ask a question that leads him or her to a different thought process. Example: "Have you considered trying..." It is easy at that point to send him or her in a new direction.

- Whether the person is right or wrong, let the team member know that you have confidence in their ability to analyze and solve the problem.

- Offer your assistance during the process, but make sure you do not assume the responsibility or do most of the work.

- Ask the person to check in with you at regular intervals so you can offer guidance or point him or her in the right direction.

- If it is a problem the team member is clearly not capable of handling, you may have to solve the problem, but make sure this person is by you every step of the way, so the next time, he or she will have the skills to handle the problem.

- In some cases, solving the problem requires interaction with the next level of management. In this situation, you may have to handle the problem, but if possible, teach this person how you solved the problem so it still becomes a learning experience.

- A great manager spots reoccurring problems and assigns the team the responsibility of making sure the problem does not occur again. Help guide their solution, but again, do not put the world on your shoulders.

People want to feel productive and they want to feel worthwhile. By letting them grow and learn you not only show great leadership and management skills, you save time and teach your team members how to become the leaders of tomorrow!

You Decide

TODAY'S WORLD CAN be overwhelming with stress at work, duties at home, raising children, attending social events, and just getting through the day. In fact, that's what most people do, they just get through the day! The question you have to ask yourself is, "Is that the life you want to live?"

Consider this simple quote by the great Albert Einstein:

"There are only two ways to live your life. One is as though nothing is a miracle. The other is as though everything is a miracle."

Sure, you can be practical and believe that this life is beyond your control, that what happens is random and you are simply a pawn in the greater scheme of the world. This way of thinking eliminates the concept of miracles. Webster's Dictionary has two definitions for miracle: A.) Wonder, B.) A supernatural happening. I like the first definition. A world filled with "wonder" has surprises and "moments of joy" around every corner. Here are a few daily "wonders:"

- A brilliant orange sunrise or sunset
- A full moon on a crystal clear cold night
- A midnight thunderstorm
- A crackling fire on a cold morning
- A baby's smile
- Giving a hug to someone you love

- Giving out a compliment to a troubled soul

- Volunteering at a homeless shelter

- Being loved

- Sending a card

This list is endless! In a real sense, each day is filled with miracles but you might be blocked from recognizing them, blinded by the emotions of anger, sorrow, fear, or worst of all self-pity.

Here is your challenge, should you choose to accept it! Start your day looking for small miracles and even more important, creating small miracles for others through a simple compliment to a stranger, a call to a long lost friend, or taking the time to tell your kids or your spouse how special they are and how much you love them. A strange thing will begin to happen, the second definition of miracles will occur, the "supernatural happening." Not the kind in movies, the kind within. You will fill with wonder and appreciation for a life well-lived for this day.

A Friendly Person

HE HAD NO reason to be as happy as he seemed. He was a doorman at a hotel in Detroit, Michigan. I passed him several times that day and each time he smiled, gave a warm greeting, and offered his assistance. It was not just me; everyone young and old got the same royal treatment, as if we were all VIP's of some sort. Some took the time to stop and chat and he would engage them in wonderful conversation. I decided to sit in the hotel lobby for a while and just observe. I liked what I saw. He not only greeted hotel guests and visitors with enthusiasm and a smile, he treated the hotel staff with the same level of courtesy and enthusiasm. After a while I decided to spend some time discovering what made this man "tick."

He was not very different from you and me. A family, friends, bills to pay, and his share of troubles filled his days. When I asked about his enthusiasm for the job, his reply was simple. "I can be here everyday and be miserable or I can be happy. I choose to be happy, not because I have to, but because I want to!" There you go. A choice! He did not believe he was one of those people born with a happy disposition, but rather he chooses to reflect energy and caring. You might argue that it was in his nature and maybe that is true, but I liked his answer just the same! Each person he encountered left a little bit better, as if a piece of this gentleman was translated within each person's heart and mind.

Michael McClung, a good friend of mine has a slogan that he feels represents who he is. It states: "Enthusiasm is contagious. I'm a carrier!" I like that! Michael "chooses" to spend his day spreading a positive attitude. You cannot help but be "infected" with his positive spirit! By the way, Michael at a very young age had a stroke. I called him a few days later in the hospital and he was his "super self." When I asked him how he felt, he replied, "I feel so blessed and lucky! So many friends have reached out to me and I feel great!" 99% of the human race would have been depressed and told their sob story, but not this special person! Having a bad day? Just call Michael and he will make you feel energized!

If you are in sales, service, or just a part of the human race, there is a magical quality about people who go through life with a positive attitude. They get along better with others, they seem to be more motivated, and their day seems to be under control. When things go badly they handle it with a positive outlook. Sure, they have their share of misfortune, what human life does not struggle at times?

I have a suspicion that they gain more customers, solve more problems in a positive way, and end the day having touched someone's life more often than not. It really does not matter what you do, doorman or doctor, loan officer or lawyer, you have a special place in the lives of your clients, patients, friends, and family, when you spread positive energy!

Want to make more sales? Want to improve your relationships with your children, spouse, clients, and colleagues? Smile more, have more positive words and thoughts on a daily basis, and make a sincere effort to touch someone in a positive way. As my friend Michael McClung would say, "Be a carrier!"

Failure...A Road to Success!

CESAR'S ANCESTORS WERE goatherds, and his father was a goat-herd. In their tiny Swiss village, there were fewer than two hundred people. His mother and father disagreed over his future. His mother had great ambitions for her son, while his father felt he should stay on the farm and tend the animals. Cesar's mother won! He was sent to school in Sion, Switzerland to learn French and mathematics. At the end of two years, he learned little of either... you see, all he wanted was to tend goats! Both parents began to worry and even his father agreed that he should do something more ambitious, so the father wrote a friend in a nearby town and actually paid the friend to hire young Cesar as a waiter in his hotel.

The boy was eager to learn and tried his best, but the more he tried, the more nervous he became. His mistakes and poor service to the hotel customers increased to such a level that the hotel manager had no choice but to fire him. He told the young boy, "You are not cut out for this type of work. Go back to the village and tend goats; that's what you were meant to do."

Cesar was heartbroken. He loved the work, but was crushed by the failure. Unable to face his parents, he did not return home but went to Paris and once again, worked in the hotel business. What happened after that is what dreams are made of! In fact, his last name is now in the dictionary! It is defined by Webster's dictionary as "elegance." The boy's last name? Ritz, Cesar Ritz, founder of the great hotel chain that has come to symbolize the best in service and luxury.

We have all felt like young Cesar Ritz. We fail or do not meet the expectations of others, and life begins a downward spiral. It was once said that it is not what happens to us in life that counts, but how we react to life's events. One person's tragedy can be another's triumph. There are few human beings who have not faced difficulty. Many have started life with disadvantages, whether physical handicaps or economic barriers. These situations can be used as crutches or building blocks. The choice is up to you.

If there is one defining talent or quality in the universe that can almost guarantee success against all odds and has lifted the most common of men and women to greatness, it is persistence. If you think about it, persistence is not really a talent; it is a state of mind, a personal decision. It is the decision to never surrender or give up regardless of what happens to us. What matters most is our reaction and our action. Persistence coupled with passion is an unstoppable force!

"Twixt failure and success the point's so fine

Men sometimes know not when they touch the line,

Just when the pearl was waiting one more plunge,

How many a struggler has thrown up the sponge!

Then take this honey from the bitterest cup:

There is no failure save in giving up!"

A Date with Destiny

Terry Shaffer wanted to give her husband David something special for the Christmas of 1977. The gift she had in mind was quite expensive for the family budget, but she was determined to give this very special gift. When she went into the little shop on Fifth Avenue in Moline, Illinois, she instantly saw what she had hoped to find. When the shopkeeper told Terry the cost, she was heartbroken since she could not afford it. The shopkeeper, sensing her disappointment, told Terry to take it and pay when she could. Terry was overjoyed.

A few weeks later, while on the nightshift, Officer David Shaffer received a call about a robbery in progress only a few blocks away. He spotted a car fitting the description of the robbery getaway car and pulled the driver over. When David approached the car, the door flew open, the suspect jumped out, and at point blank range, the suspect fired a 45 caliber round into the abdomen of David Shaffer. The young wife got the fateful call. Her husband had been shot. Terry hung up the phone and a smile of joy and relief overwhelmed her. It seems that David Shaffer was saved by a very special gift from his very loving wife. Terry had bought him a bulletproof vest for Christmas! His date with destiny had been delayed. Was it fate or was it the love of a wife and the generosity of a shopkeeper? It does not matter. Tragedy became triumph!

So often, we want to assign some reason to the negative events in our life. We blame it on destiny or fate. In truth, what happens to us, in most cases, occurs from a series of decisions and actions all leading to a crossroad of triumph or tragedy. It is true that we cannot control the actions of a drunk driver or a natural disaster. But even in these events, it is the series of decisions and actions after the event that adds significance to our life or puts us on a tailspin of sadness and depression. MADD, Mothers Against Drunk Drivers, was formed by a mother who lost her child in a head-on collision with a drunk driver. The "Make a Wish Foundation" was formed by a parent who lost her child to cancer and was able to fulfill a final wish for him. Out of these tragedies came countless lives saved, strong legislation against drunk driving, and thousands of children realizing the dreams of a lifetime in the worst of circumstances. Charles A. Hall said,

"We sow our thoughts, and we reap our action;
We sow our actions, and we reap our habits;
We sow our habits and we reap our character;
We sow our character and we reap our destiny."

Let no man or woman say, "Why did this happen to me?" Instead, let him or her say, "How can I make the best happen?" The world will give you what you ask if you truly believe and are willing to take action on those beliefs. Everyone has a tragedy to tell, but only a few have the honor and distinction to tell a story of triumph out of their tragedy. Live to win!

The Finishers

IN THE SEMI-FINALS of the 1992 Olympic 400 meters Great Britain's Derek Redmond was guaranteed to finish in the top four and make the Olympic finals. With 175 meters left in the race, tragedy struck and Derek Redmond fell to the track in pain from a severe muscle pull. It would have been easy to quit the race, but Redmond rose to his feet and began hopping the long and painful path around the track. In a moment that would never be forgotten in Olympic history, someone came to his aid, Derek Redmond's father. Together, arm-in-arm, they finished the race. You see, Derek Redmond and his father were "finishers."

Maybe life is really about finishing. When I take the time to examine the accomplishments of great people there is one thing they all have in common, they are "finishers." How often have people attended a seminar, discovered a great idea, started to implement, but never finished? That great idea for a novel? You know the story. An average idea fully implemented is far better than a great idea never started.

Why do so many people fail to finish what they start? The answer is not an easy one and is often different for each person, but we can trace most failure to finish to a few key elements.

- Loss of enthusiasm- So often someone starts a great project and after a short time, when a few obstacles get in the way and there are no quick results, the enthusiasm leaves, and the project goes unfinished. Solution- Prepare for obstacles by anticipating hardships and planning how to overcome them.

- Get rich quick mentality- We live in a society that demands everything now, I call it the disease of "instantitis." When success is not reached easily people simply quit and wait for the next "get rich quick" scheme. Solution- Expect anything worthwhile to take time and effort. If you are not willing to put in the work, outsource what you will not do yourself.

- Daily action- A series of small actions achieved daily are far more powerful that a few giant steps. This might be one of the biggest reasons for failure to finish. Daily action takes a daily plan. Most people let their day run them rather than running their day. Solution- The last thing at night or first thing in the morning write your action steps for your important project and keep those steps in front of you the entire day.

- Choosing the right partners- In the Olympic 400 meters Derek Redmond had his father. Successful people are willing to enlist the help of others to reach their goals and dreams. Solution- When successful people start a project, they look for the best talent possible to assist the endeavor.

- Loving what you do- Most people have never found their passion in life. It is so much easier to finish if you love what you start. Never begin a project that your heart and soul does not yearn to finish. Solution- Never be afraid to reach for the stars!

There is no limit, no measure to the size of the human heart when it beats to the sound of a dream and refuses to ever stop beating! Live to laugh, live to learn, live to dream, but most of all, live to win!

The Real Story

ONE OF THE immortal moments in sports was Lou Gehrig's farewell speech given on July 4th, 1939 in front of 80,000 fans in Yankee Stadium. Baseball's "Ironman" was dying of a dreaded degenerative muscular disease that even today bears his name. When he stepped to the microphone, his first words were, "Today, I consider myself the luckiest man on the face of the earth!" Most believed he was talking about his fame and the warm outpouring of the crowd, but the true meaning of his words began two years earlier.

When the Yankees were playing the White Sox in Chicago, Lou received an urgent plea from the parents of a ten year-old boy, stricken with polio. In a state of depression, the boy refused to participate in any form of therapy to restore his ability to walk. Lou visited the young boy, told him that he wanted the boy to walk again, and pleaded with the child to go to therapy. The boy replied, "If you hit a homerun for me, I'll go to therapy!" Gehrig not only hit a homerun; he hit two! He felt a deep sense of obligation to inspire the young boy named Tim.

More than two years later and on that memorable day in July 1939, an event took place before Lou Gehrig approached the microphone to give his heartfelt farewell speech. Little Tim, now twelve years old, came out of the Yankee dugout, dropped his crutches, and walked into the outstretched arms of baseball's greatest hero. They hugged and cried. A twelve year-old boy inspired the true meaning of Lou Gehrig's farewell words!

The acts of kindness and sacrifice we perform for others truly make all of us the luckiest people on the face of the earth. We may not be famous like Lou Gehrig, but we have the same opportunity to change lives with our kindness and our focus on others. Let no day pass without performing little acts of kindness. These acts of kindness are contagious. Each time you perform one, encourage the recipient to pass it on and do the same. If only a few actually do so the world would be a much better place. John Dunne wrote:

"No man is an island,
Entire of itself.
Each is a piece of the continent,
A part of the main."

We are all a part of humanity, each responsible in some way for the other. In truth the final words of John Dunne's passage says it best regarding our responsibility:

"Each man's death diminishes me,
For I am involved in mankind.
Therefore, send not to know
For whom the bell tolls,
It tolls for thee."

Garages of Destiny

WHAT DO 10704 NE 28th St., Bellevue, Washington, 2066 Crist Dr. Los Altos, California, 4651 Kingswell Ave., Los Angeles, California, 232 Santa Margarita Ave., Menlo Park, California and 367 Addison Ave., Palo Alto, California all have in common? They are all the addresses where businesses were started in garages. Lack of funding, lack of backers, and only dreams, these addresses were the hopes of young dreamers and a hope for a better tomorrow. Let's take a closer look and walk inside these "garages of destiny."

- NE 28th Street was the home of one of the first online bookstores founded by one man in 1994. In 1995 the company sold its first book and two years later issued its IPO. Jeff Bezos founded Amazon.com, today the world's largest online retailer.

- 2066 Crist Drive housed the dream of two twenty-something nerds. In 1976 they sold their first home and built computers to a local retailer. Unfortunately, the two didn't have enough money to complete the order so they took the purchase order to a parts distributor and got an advance to build their 50 computers in 30 days. Steve Jobs and Steve Wozniak founded Apple Computer in that small garage.

- 4651 Kingswell Ave. actually belonged to the two brothers' uncle, Robert. The boys used the one car separate garage to film their first cartoon production of the Alice Comedies, which was part of the original Alice's Wonderland. Walt and

Roy Disney never gave up, even through several bankruptcies, to build the Disney empire, the highest grossing media conglomerate in the world.

- 367 Addison Ave. was the starting point for two engineers who had a dream of starting their own company. Their first product was an audio oscillator and one of their first customers was Walt Disney Studios. This "HP Garage" was known at the birthplace of Silicon Valley and Hewlett-Packard grew to one of the largest companies in the world. Thank you Bill Hewlett and Dave Packard for rounding up $538.00 to make your first instrument!

- 232 Santa Margarita Ave. was actually a borrowed garage of Susan Wojcicki. Larry and Sergey were two young Stanford University graduate students who had what they thought was an incredible idea of building a search engine for the Internet based on a formula they had created. Soon the project was interfering with their graduate studies so they tried to sell their idea to Excite for one million dollars. Excite rejected the offer and now Google is the most trafficked site in the world!

How many great ideas have you had over the course of your lifetime? We are all amazingly talented in some way and we all have a passion about something whether it is sports, baking, or writing. At the five addresses above, someone took action on their passion and in most cases it was after numerous failures and setbacks. Here is a quote to remember, "The distance between a great idea and turning it into a success can be traced to the length of the trail of sweat drops and tear drops."

We could add a thousand more addresses and a thousand more garages and the stories would be the same, never giving up on a dream and finding a way to the path of success. There is no failure in falling. The failing is not getting up after you fall.

Critics Don't Count

HAVE YOU EVER wondered how someone becomes a critic? Is there a level of expertise that is beyond the normal human capability? Is there a school somewhere that teaches certain people how to point out what is wrong? Certainly there are many critics who spread positive words along with most of the negative feedback that exists in the world. The really unfortunate thing in life is that some people actually take critics seriously and even believe what they say. Countless egos have been shattered by criticism while rare individuals rise above the negative feedback and only try harder to reach success.

The great American President, Theodore Roosevelt once said, "It is not the critic who counts. Not the one who showed how the strong man stumbled or how the doer of a deed could have done better. The credit goes to the man who is actually in the arena, whose face is marred with dust and sweat and blood. Who errs and falls short again and again. Who knows the great enthusiasms, the great devotions and who spends himself in a worthy cause. At the best, he knows the triumph of high achievement and at the worst, if he fails, at least fails while striving valiantly so his place shall never be among those cold and timid souls who know neither victory nor defeat."

Criticism is not a bad thing. We can grow and learn from our mistakes, but as with most things in life, it is not always what we do, but how we do it that is so crucial. If you are in a position to criticize others, do it with kindness and make sure you offer your support. Revel in the success of others, give credit quickly, and praise warmly and with enthusiasm whether it is a small child or a grandmother. The world has a special reward for the positive people and leaders of this earth. That reward is a special vision that allows them to look into the heart of others and believe in the goodness that exists, while ignoring the brief failings. These are the truly contented people on this planet and happiness enters their lives every day in small and large ways.

The great inspirational writer Dale Carnegie once said, "Any fool can criticize, condemn, and complain, and most fools do!" Take time today to praise someone and if there is the opportunity to find fault instead, find the opportunity to search deeper and find goodness!

It is impossible to calculate the number of people who never initiated a great idea or who never put their dream into action because of critics, whether well-meaning loved ones or one of the numerous negative individuals that have never achieved anything themselves but are quick to point out the faults of others. Here is a novel idea, call it a challenge. This evening in the calm of night take out a piece of paper and write down what you would do with your life knowing that you could not fail. Put that piece of paper under your pillow and sleep on it. In the morning take it out and look at what you wrote. Does it still have the same impact on you as when you wrote it the night before? If so, take one step toward your dream. Maybe you research the topic or you take one step by writing the first page of your novel. Whatever the dream, only many small actions can make it come to life. Good luck on your journey to your dreams! By the way, on your journey there will be numerous critics...ignore them!

211 Degrees

WATER MAY BE the most incredible substance on the face of the earth! It is composed of the simplest of elements, two parts hydrogen and one part oxygen. Separate, each is a gas, one that ignites and burns at high temperatures and one that is necessary for fires to continue burning as the flames consume oxygen. Miraculously, when combined in the right way, the gases form water which puts out most fires! Is that crazy?

Water is used to heat homes, cook food, and at the other end of the scale when turned to ice preserves food, cools homes, and even turns to snow for a beautiful winter landscape. It may be the most important substance on the face of the earth for life cannot be sustained without water. When water is cooled below 32 degrees Fahrenheit it is a solid, but here is the real "power of water." If you heat water to 211 degrees Fahrenheit, you have very hot water! It can be used for many things, but when you heat it one more degree, it boils and turns to steam. That steam can run steam driven engines in locomotives or giant turbines to produce electricity for an entire city or state. Just that one degree of difference releases all the power of one of the simplest, most harmless substances on the earth and suddenly unleashes limitless power with just a one degree change!

What about you? Has your life been set at 211 degrees? Have you had great ideas, but never put them into reality? Did you start a book, a project, or a dream but never saw it through? If you have, you are like so many people. You have many uses and skills, just like water, but you have never fully unleashed your power! To raise the water one degree is a simple thing, but how do you do it with a human being? The answer is enthusiasm.

It is the flame that heats the soul! Intelligence is a wonderful and powerful thing, but intelligence without a passion, without a desire, is simply thinking, not doing. It is enthusiasm alone that brings the human soul to the boiling point where all its power is unleashed and the impossible becomes the probable.

I do not know if I have ever found the person who does not have a passion about something. It could be comic books or chemistry, it really does not matter. Whatever it is—provided it serves a worthy cause—can be turned to greatness. Stan Lee was one of the founders of Marvel Comics. His passion for comic books created Spiderman, The X-Men and many other superheroes and villains that have been turned into movies and are known worldwide.

Mrs. Fields had a passion, an enthusiasm for baking chocolate chip cookies. Her passion made her a well-known millionaire! Do not shortchange yourself because you view yourself as untalented or un-skilled, there is no such thing! Even in the worst of circumstances people have refused to give up on their dreams, their passion. So no excuses are permitted!

The great minister and writer, Dr. Robert Shuler once said, "What dreams would you dare to dream if you knew you could not fail?" The answer to that question would create the ultimate enthusiasm. It would be your ultimate dream! Where are you today? What is your state of mind? What gets you up in the morning and allows you to give your best every day? Find it. And do it.

But do it with enthusiasm!

Monday, Monday

IT'S YOUR OFFICE day. You know, the day you are supposed to be planning ahead, strategizing, and getting all those appointments made for the coming weeks. The truth is in today's environment you are on the phone putting out fires all day long. An office day can make you incredibly productive or it can be a wasted opportunity. Using your office day wisely can put you back on track quickly and grow your business or it can be a day of frustration. Let' look at how the office day can be a key to your success.

The true purpose of an office day is to spend time in tasks that make you more productive. That means having a routine and setting goals for what you want to accomplish on your office day. Here is what I recommend to all our coaching clients.

1.   Start early! If you can start your office day around 7 a.m. (depending on when the kids get up, maybe earlier!) you can do your most important tasks first before the interruptions begin. There are several tasks that lead to increased production that should be priorities. (see next few items)

2.   Review your territory sectors. You should have your accounts divided into geographic sectors of five accounts in each sector. These accounts should be ranked from the best to the worst and decisions should be made on each sector for the month, such as:

"Which accounts should be eliminated?"

"Which sales calls will lead to the most business?"

"Who needs to be managed for better pull through or quality?"

3.   Review your top 25 relationships also, ranked from the best to the merely good!

"Which loan officers should you see?"

"Who did you miss on your last call to an office?"

"Which of these loan officers are abusing the system and need to be managed?"

"Which loan officers need to be rewarded?"

"Who needs a thank you card or a thank you email?"

"Which relationships do I need to take to the next level this month?"

4.   Any marketing that needs to go out for the week should be done in this first hour. I send an economic update to my clients each month for them to distribute to their clients.

5.   Decide who you need to make an appointment with in order to have a productive sales call. Many AE's tell me "Ken, I don't make appointments, they know me!" My answer to that is no matter how well they know you, if you "drop in" and they are not there it is a wasted trip. Professionals make appointments!

6.   Set your goals for the week with the most important ones to be accomplished first. Decide which day you will accomplish the goal and just do it!

If you just get these things done, you will be so far ahead of the game and the stress and pressure you usually feel will begin to disappear. Lack of productivity is the biggest reason for failure in sales and also the biggest reason for burnout. You cannot afford to lose this valuable day to lack of organization, excuse making, and poor planning. Your success depends upon it! Charles Bixton said, "You will never find time for anything. If you want time, you must make it!"

The Race of Life

JOHN BAKER WAS a middle distance runner on the University of New Mexico's track team. As one of the nation's top milers, he was destined to fulfill his dream of becoming a future Olympic hopeful. After graduation, he began coaching at Aspen Elementary School in his hometown of Albuquerque, New Mexico. While on a training run one day, he fell to his knees with pain in his chest and abdomen. Exploratory surgery revealed terminal cancer that had spread throughout his body. The doctors gave him less than six months to live.

John had a choice to make. Would he fall into a depression and curse the unfairness of life, or would he make the most of the time he had left? He decided to devote the rest of his life to children. In addition to his duties at Aspen Elementary, John helped his best friend, John Haaland, coach the Duke City Dashers, a small track club for girls from elementary school through high school. He spent endless hours teaching not only athletic skills but skills for life as well.

One of the athletes had a younger sister who wore a leg brace. John spent as much time with her as he did with any of the "stars." He taught them self-worth, not based upon their talent but their efforts. He gave medals to the "triers" as well as the winners. Who were the triers? They were the girls who never won or even placed in the meets but gave a supreme effort at the meets and in practice. Incidentally, the medals John gave them were from his many championships as a great athlete. These treasures of his life were given as a token from his heart. The Duke City Dashers did so well that they qualified for the

AAU National Championships!

John Baker's race was over shortly thereafter. He died as he had lived: as a true champion. After his death, the community changed the name of Aspen Elementary to John Baker Elementary as a memorial to a courageous and giving spirit. So many lives touched, so many dreams achieved. He was a shining example of winning.

Author Michael Roemer wrote, "We die as we have lived; we bring to this last great act of our lives whatever we have brought to earlier acts. In this sense, we can't really learn to die; we can only learn to live."

Perhaps the greatest gift you can give to anyone is the gift of yourself. As humans, we all have the wonderful talent of spreading kindness. Whether to a co-worker, a small child, the elderly, or a person on the streets, every smile, every hello, and every kind word we give them takes seed and grows in the human heart."

For just one day, try this: live a day of giving. Take the time to say hello to strangers, compliment someone in the workplace, tell your spouse something you appreciate about him or her, let your customers know how important they are, or tell a child something positive about him or herself. At the end of that day, take a moment to reflect on how it made you feel and what it did for others. The greatest gifts of life are the little things we do. And these seeds of kindness grow into wondrous things.

There is a Santa Claus

"DEAR SANTA, MY name is Val and I have a four-and-a-half-year-old brother. His name is Jonathan and we live with our Mom. I need to ask you for something very important. We do not have any money this Christmas and my little brother needs a coat. He is a size 10. If you can please get one for him, my Mom and myself would be forever grateful. P.S. Thank you. We love you, Santa."

Every year children write letters to Santa Claus addressed to the North Pole. Over sixty years ago, when these letters arrived in the New York City area, a few dedicated postal workers decided these letters should not go unanswered. They began answering the letters with return addresses and even sending gifts to needy children in the New York area. Over the years, the number of letters continued to grow and in this year over 100,000 letters are expected! The New York Post Office appealed to the public for volunteers to assist in answering the letters and Operation Santa Claus was born. A computer system insures that no letters are answered twice and great care is given to assist the children who are in the greatest need. The letter from Val is just one example of needy kids who are helped every year by postal workers and volunteers in the New York area. Many of the letters ask for nothing more than hope and an answer from the jolly old elf and the New Yorkers in the program make sure that every child gets an answer.

"Dear Santa, I often wonder, is there something that makes miracles, because I know you exist and my family believes in you. Not for presents, but only for those who try to make something out of themselves. I believe in you because I know you would do so much for my family.

Please Santa, give my family anything that would make them feel happy. I really don't want anything for myself, just my family, because I love them. Thanks Santa, for listening, really." This letter was from a 15-year-old boy asking only for hope and for others.

Some of the letters come from homeless families in shelters, others from children of families who have met with difficulties from lost jobs to homes burning down during the year. Each letter is a symbol of the hope and faith of each child, even in the worst of circumstances that a small request will be answered, even if it is just for a reply and reassurance that there is a brighter day.

Post offices all over America have started special programs and many have started programs similar to the New York Central Post Office. Want to make a difference this Holiday Season? Contact your local post office and ask about any volunteer programs, or if they receive any "Letters to Santa." Maybe this will be your greatest Christmas ever because you reached out beyond your world and into the hopes and dreams of a small child? We wish a happy holiday season to you, our clients, and a hope that this special time of year will find you in wonderful spirits and touching the lives of those around you!

Life Isn't Fair

WHY ME? HOW did Bob get the promotion that I deserved? After all I have been here longer and have worked harder! How does Mary get so lucky? All the really big deals always come her way! This company doesn't have the right products or I would be more successful! Why don't we have a construction perm program? I could really sell that product! I can't believe I didn't invest in that stock when I had the chance! Why do some people seem to have all the luck? As we search for the reasons some people are more successful, it always seems to come back to the "unfairness of life." Let's get this out of the way upfront. Life is neither fair nor unfair, it is just life! Good and bad happens and some people get a disproportionate amount of the bad. Life being unfair is really not the problem. The problem is when we buy into that belief. When you choose to accept the fact that life is unfair and you are "the victim," well…you are the victim of your own making. Some people seem to have their "unfair" share of life. Let's look at a few:

- Thomas Edison was called "stupid" when he was young and to a great degree was self-educated. Why? He had a severe hearing handicap.

- Beethoven suffered from a total loss of hearing…and produced some of his best music after the fact.

- Walt Disney went bankrupt several times. After losing everything three times over, he created the first animated cartoon.

- The great baseball legend Babe Ruth grew up in an orphanage.

- Alexander the Great died at the age of 38…after he conquered the known world.

- Ray Charles wasn't born blind, he lost his sight while a young boy.

Yes, life isn't fair. No one ever promised it would be fair. It is most unfair to those who acquire the attitude of "what's the use in trying." At that point, life loses a little of it's luster and excitement. Every day is spent waiting for the next "unfair" event. Guess what? It happens! You see, what you believe to be true in your world is true, at least in your mind. And the mind is a powerful thing. It can shape and create our own future and destiny. So, what is your thinking like? Are you waiting for the next unlucky event to enter your life? Are you waiting to complain about the unfairness of life? Let me share a story with you…

I know a man whose father committed suicide when the boy was six. Six months later he lost the sight in his right eye due to an accident. When he was a boy the family lost everything they had when their house burned to the ground. A little embarrassed, he wore donated clothes to school. All of his grandparents died before he reached the age of thirteen. His mother died of cancer when he was twelve and he was moved around from relative to relative. Too poor to pay for college, his only hope was a scholarship. His first child was born handicapped and he almost went bankrupt following his dream to be a professional speaker. Who is that man? That man is me.

No, my life was not fair, but I learned early that things happen for reasons we cannot always fathom. What is important is this… each day you approach your life with a renewed excitement. Each day you set goals and make dreams. Each day you try to touch someone in a positive way.

Don't Ever Give Up!

HE HAD A dream and refused to quit. When Jim Valvano graduated from Rutgers University, he knew he wanted to be a basketball coach. By the age of twenty-three, Jim was head coach at John Hopkins, a school that had not had a winning season in twenty-five years. Coach Valvano took them to a winning season his first year. In 1980, at the age of thirty-four, Valvano became head basketball coach at North Carolina State University. In 1983, the team made it to the NCAA National Championship game against Houston. According to the national press, and most other coaches, the game was a total mismatch and NC State did not have a chance. They won at the buzzer 54-52!

Coach Valvano went on to become a top sports announcer for ESPN. In June of 1992, he began the toughest battle of his life: bone cancer. Though filled with pain, he refused to quit and continued his career while fighting for his life. His motto to his players had always been, "Don't give up. Don't ever give up!"

In March of 1993, at the American Sports Award ceremony, Jim Valvano was honored to receive the Arthur Ashe Award for Courage. He reached the podium in a wheelchair and was assisted to his feet. His message was brief and powerful. He said, "There are three things you should do in life every day. Number one is laugh. Number two is think. Spend time in deep thought. And number three is let your emotions move you to tears. If you laugh, think, and cry out of joy, that's a heck of a day!" His final words were, "Never give up. Don't ever give up!"

Jim Valvano died in April of that year, but not before inspiring thousands of cancer patients and starting the Jimmy V. Foundation for cancer research. His message is not about dying with courage; it is about living. Each day provides for us a choice. We can choose to feel sorry for ourselves or we can choose to live with courage. We can choose to laugh or to be sad. We can choose to take the negatives in our life and let them overwhelm us or we can fight with courage and conviction to create victory out of defeat.

Everyone has a Jim Valvano somewhere in his or her heart. The history of the world is the history of ordinary men and women doing extraordinary things. Coach V. was an ordinary man with extraordinary courage and conviction. Whatever you face, you can face it with self-pity or you can face it with courage. Choose courage and your life will change forever! Never give up. Don't ever give up!

Overnight Success

JACK NICHOLSON WON the Academy Award for Best Actor in his portrayal of an obsessive-compulsive individual in "As Good As It Gets." This made him the most honored actor in film history, with three academy awards and twelve nominations. It is easy to look at someone like Jack Nicholson and think, "Wow, what a natural talent!" But, like most successful people, Nicholson, too, has a story to share.

Jack went to Hollywood at the age of 17 with one dream: to be an actor. For twelve years, his career went nowhere as he struggled to make ends meet by working odd jobs and acting in "B" grade movies. He considered himself lucky when he got a bit part on the "Divorce Court" TV show. His first big hit was not until he was 32 years old in the movie "Easy Rider." He said he was willing to risk his 20's on his dream. All this time, he took his work seriously, diligently learning and perfecting his skills, including writing six screen plays, co-producing three movies, and editing five.

Whenever Nicholson gets a part in a movie, he immediately begins memorizing not only his lines, but everyone else's. He breaks the script down to 3" X 5" cards and underlines every key word to practice the emotion and emphasis. In "One Flew Over the Cuckoo's Nest," he spent time mingling with patients in an asylum and even watched while they received shock therapy. The superintendent of the asylum said Nicholson was a genius in the role of McMurphy, a sociopath. He won the Oscar for Best Actor for his role.

In the movie "Ironwood," Nicholson played the part of a derelict. In preparation, he spent time lying face down in a public restroom, next to the toilets to get the feeling of hopelessness and despair.

Nicholson studied numerous acting styles throughout his career to capture the essence of any role from comedy to drama. When asked about his success, he said, "I can't do anything else but act. I have to give my life to this job!"

Overnight success? Sheer talent? Lucky? Right place at the right time? These are excuses we use when explaining the success of others. You only have to look at a Jack Nicholson to discover the true essence of success.

First, he had a dream, just as everyone does. However, Jack Nicholson did one thing different than most. He took action! At 17 years old, he went to a strange town, with no job and no leads, only a dream.

Second, he pursued his dream with a passion. It was not enough to be good or better than someone else. He wanted to be better than himself, to go beyond the limits of his own talents. Hard work does this; it grows the muscles of our mind and allows us to exceed our wildest expectations.

The great playwright George Bernard Shaw said, "You see things: and you say why? But I dream things that never were, and I say why not?" This brings us to the final question, "So what's holding you back?" There are no excuses. Only action. So, what are you waiting for?

The Hidden Leader

It is easy to spot "perceived leaders." They are the ones with titles like vice president, CEO, or manager. I use the word perceived because a title is no guarantee that a person is a true leader. Often the real leaders in an organization are hidden, but their acts of leadership make a difference every day. They don't ask to be recognized, they don't expect a raise for their contribution and they act not out of a sense of obligation, but out of a sense of opportunity. These hidden leaders bring a special attitude to their work and to their lives that are examples of the true qualities of leadership. Now I raise the real question, what makes them leaders if they, in many cases, have no one to lead? The answer is simple, true leaders perform the most difficult task of leading people over whom they have no authoritative power. They are "titleless" but not "powerless."

I offer an interesting and thought provoking definition of leadership. A true leader has the gift of inspiring others to achieve great things through the leader's genuine desire to make a difference in the lives of people and organizations. This does not require a title; it requires a very specific set of skills:

- An unselfish desire to make a difference- They act for the good of others, not for the benefit of self.

- An attitude of "opportunity" rather than obligation- If we feel obligated to do something we perform out of guilt or necessity. The hidden leader looks at tasks and sees a greater purpose and is thus motivated to exceed expectations.

- The ability to communicate with others in a way that makes others excited about contributing and helping even when they are not obligated to do so (opportunity!).

- A willingness to give more than they expect- As a result they get far more than they expect. The "Law of Abundance" applies to the hidden leader. This law states there is plenty to go around whether praise (they give it sincerely and often) or guidance (they give it, but it ways that uplift others).

- A drive to always do their very best at any task no matter how menial- The hidden leader is motivated by quality—not quantity—of work and performs tasks perfectly and to completion.

Here is the problem, often "titled leaders" do not recognize the hidden leaders until it is too late and they have either left the organization to make a difference somewhere else or another department internally recognizes their talent and offers a better opportunity. The task of people in positions of authority is to constantly be alert to hidden leaders, praise them, and promote them. That means spending less time managing and more time leading based on the five skills above.

"A leader is best when people barely know he exists, when his work is done, his aim fulfilled, they will say: we did it ourselves."

Lao Tzu

A Cut Above

Over the many years I have been consulting with corporations and sales organizations I have been able to identify a key set of traits that the best of the best corporations and individuals possess which set them apart. They are a "cut above." Let's start with the corporations. As you read this think about your own organization and also the many customers in your marketplace.

Top organizations are focused on their customers. They reflect this focus by doing the following:

- Going the extra mile in understanding the customers' needs and adapting to meet those needs. My best definition of a need is simply a problem that requires a solution. Going the extra mile means thinking outside of the box and finding solutions.

- Great companies have a relentless focus on customer service. It is not about what is convenient for the company, it is what is convenient for the customer. These great companies relentlessly train their team members to handle every situation. They are relentless in response time and populating their ranks with knowledgeable employees.

- They are constantly recruiting top talent and once recruited making sure team members are appreciated and supported.

- Great companies have great leadership. My best definition of great leadership is the leader who provides a clear vision for his or her team and then allows team members to perform by clearing obstacles in their path.

- These organizations are "sales-centric." They have the clear understanding that the success of any company is based on the strength of its sales force. These sales teams are well trained, have clear goals, and are empowered to make decisions.

- Top organizations are willing to take calculated risk. They understand that the world changes quickly and they must adapt in how they do business. What worked yesterday could put you out of business today. Constant change is the mark of excellence.

- Finally, the best organizations create a pride in their organization by honoring their team members and recognizing performance. Team members, in turn, are willing to go the extra mile in performing their jobs.

How difficult is it to become the best of the best? Probably a better question would be … is a company willing to pay the price to be the best?

If you are a current leader in an organization, a great exercise would be to rate yourself 1 through 5 in each of the categories above with 1 being poor and 5 being superior. If you don't score at least a 38 you have a lot of work to do. Roll up your sleeves and get to work. It's never too late.

The Extra Mile

THE YOUNG RISING country star, Lonzo Green, was in town visiting relatives and no one was more proud than his teenage nephew Jimmy. Jimmy spread the word at school, but Lonzo was somewhat surprised when he found out that one of Jimmy's friends was not allowed in their home. Jimmy's parents felt the teenage boy was "from the wrong side of the tracks" and might be a bad influence. The young friend, however, had a request. He wanted to know if Jimmy's cousin Lonzo would help tune his guitar. He was just learning to play, but had no idea how to adjust his new instrument. Jimmy's parents relented somewhat after his pleas and allowed Jimmy's friend to stop by, but he must stay outside, and he could not stay for long.

As the young boy approached, Lonzo noticed the timid glances and insecurities, but also the very humble nature of this boy from "the wrong side of the tracks." They shook hands and the teenage boy smiled. He asked the young man if anyone hand ever taught him how to tune his guitar and in a slow and polite Southern drawl he answered, "No, sir." Lonzo carefully showed him how to tune the guitar and when he finished, the boy thanked him and got up to leave. Lonzo would not let him go! He too had grown up in poverty and knew how a little kindness could mean so much to a shy teenager from the "wrong side of the tracks."

The late afternoon light faded and one song led to another as the boy's shyness was replaced by his love of music and a stranger's kindness. Lonzo and the young boy would never meet again. For his part the young man left with a warm memory and encouragement from a stranger who took time to care. The young boy never forgot the kindness, not through thirty-three motion pictures and over four hundred million records sold. That warm summer afternoon so long ago gave a young boy encouragement that would forever touch his heart. That young man was Elvis Presley.

Life is filled with opportunities. Some of the greatest opportunities are those that touch another human life in a kind and gracious way. Maybe your volunteer work at the local Boys and Girls Club encouraged one young girl to seek a career in medicine and ultimately discover a cure for cancer! Maybe your kindness to a stranger allowed him or her to regain belief in the goodness of people! William Wordsworth said, "The best portion of a good man's life is his little, nameless, unremembered acts of kindness and of love." Each act of kindness spreads its wave throughout human eternity. The greatest among us is that man or woman who is never diminished by the success and happiness of others and proves it by random acts of kindness and the power of a sincere and caring smile! Go the extra mile. You will be glad you did!

Never Discount an Idea!

IN LATE 1978, the engineers at Sony were disappointed. Previously they had created an extremely popular miniature recording device called the "Pressman" which became the standard for journalist around the world. The problem was the Pressman was in mono and the news journalist wanted one in stereo. The engineers were able to fit the stereo speakers and the playback device, but the recording mechanism would not fit in the small casing! One day Masara Ibuka, one of the original founders of Sony, happened to walk into the lab where the Pressman improvements were at a standstill. Ibuka was a little eccentric and no longer fit into the day-to-day operations of Sony, so he had been appointed honorary chairman—merely a ceremonial title. He spent his days wandering the halls of the corporation. When he saw and heard the stereo Pressman excitement bubbled within him! Ibuka had been in another department where he had seen and tested a great pair of headphones. "Why don't you take the speakers out of the Pressman? It would make a great music player!" he exclaimed. Unaware of the headphones and unimpressed with Ibuka's idea, they forged ahead. "Who would want to listen to music through headphones," they thought? Ibuka, with no authority to make any decisions, went to his co-founder, now president of Sony, Akio Morita and showed him the device with headphones. Morita was so impressed with the sound that he ordered the project to begin!

Now, it was the marketing department who thought the idea would never work, but based on Morita's orders they pressed on. In Japan the device was called the "Walkman" but in America it was marketed as the "Soundabout," and the marketing efforts were focused toward teenagers. The product did not sell! The marketing department was right, at least temporarily. Yuppies soon discovered the device, however, and the rest is history. To this day the Walkman is one of Sony's greatest achievements.

What is the lesson in all of this? If companies would communicate internally and cooperate, so much more could be achieved! The larger a company becomes the more opposed it becomes to innovation and new ideas. Leaders with a vision like Ibuka are needed to push corporations to be creative and continue to innovate. Too often in today's corporate world, there are people afraid to take chances. Embrace change, be willing to take calculated risk, do not give up on ideas and most of all ... never lose "big picture thinking." The results will amaze you!

Have you got that idea in your head that you have never acted upon? Have you wanted to start your own business or embark on a new career? Breaking out of the "conformity mold" is not easy, but with the right plan, the right passion, and the right purpose, nothing is impossible.

Writing Your Own Ending

THERE IS NOTHING like a great story, especially when it has a great ending! The intrigue, the excitement, and the mystery only seem to matter when the story has an ending that captures our minds. Every life is a story. We are the authors of our own plot. Many people live life as if someone else were writing their life story. This causes individuals to relinquish control to some mysterious force. No one can write your story better than you!

A great ending starts with a great story line and a great plot. Your story line could be "Average person lives a life of daily existence hoping for retirement one day" or it could be "Human being with a dream focuses on achieving it against all odds!" The usual plot is pretty simple. A person works very hard every day and somehow cannot seem to get ahead. Roadblock after roadblock appears and each one takes a small piece of the dream until it becomes a distant, unattainable star.

It is never too late to stop the presses before the final chapters of your life are written! All of the past failures and obstacles only serve as a great beginning to an amazing story of triumph. Let's look at that storyline one more time. "Human being with a dream uses life's tragedies and hardships to never give up and ultimately achieve beyond their wildest dreams." Now, that's a life story worth reading! Is it that difficult to believe it can happen? The answer of course is, "No." Anyone can write that story! Here are the steps:

- A great author starts with the simplest plan: daily effort. A novelist writes every day, even when he or she does not feel like writing. The writer of his or her own life must do the same. The dream has to be lived and acted upon daily with unrelenting action.

- The author researches to make the story as accurate and believable as possible. The author of his or her own life researches the dream and gathers all the tools to make it possible. Whether those tools are education, experience, or seeking the knowledge of others, it is a never-ending quest.

- The great writer focuses upon life experiences to make the book come alive. Every hardship serves to create a new story and idea to enrich every word on the pages. The author of his or her own life does the same. Every failure becomes a wonderful subplot in overcoming obstacles and turning them into triumph.

- The author fills the story with people who all have an essential part in making the story come alive. The "life author" realizes that without positive influences to help him or her along the way, each chapter would be difficult to complete. The positive people in our lives only give us more energy to reach the dream.

- The great writer is passionate about every word, every chapter, and wants to make it the best! So it is with stories of triumph and the people who live them!

What about your life story? Is the grind of life filling the pages with stories and incidents that seem beyond your control or have you made the decision to take life's obstacles and use them as material to create the great American novel? "Human being reaches wildest dreams against all odds, proving the power of the human spirit." Everyone will want an autographed copy!

The Law of Explosive Growth!

IN 1984, AT the age of 22, John Schnatter started his own business. He began selling pizzas out of a converted broom closet in his father's tavern. John had vision, determination, and a strong work ethic. By the beginning of 1991, he had opened 46 stores. That is a tremendous success story in itself. By the end of 1992, he had 1600 locations throughout the nation! What was the key to the dramatic growth in only two years? John found the secret to explosive growth!

In the early years, John Schnatter was the leader. He spent most of his time focused on his ability to create motivation and enthusiasm in his team. In early 1991, he realized that he had really missed the secret. Instead of using his energy to excite and motivate his employees, he needed to focus on hiring and developing great leaders that would multiply his efforts a hundred fold. First he hired Wade Oney who helped create Domino's Pizza's great success. In turn, each leader he hired and nurtured brought on more leaders. They understood the difference between "follower's math" and "leader's math." Leaders who develop followers grow their team or organization one person at a time. Leaders who develop leaders magnify growth tenfold! It is the difference between addition and multiplication.

Organizations make disastrous errors when they do not continually develop their leadership and focus that leadership on hiring not just the best sales people or operations people, but those individuals who also exhibit the best leadership skills. Here is a checklist:

____ 1. Do you continually train your leaders in the skills of leadership?

If not, you have a false sense of security.

___ 2. When hiring, do you focus solely on the skill to do the job such as sales success, or do you look beyond the basic skills to leadership skills?

___ 3. Do you continually support their freedom to make crucial leadership decisions, or is it controlled centrally?

___ 4. Do you bog down your leaders with so much detail and reporting that they do not have time to lead and develop leaders?

___ 5. Have you trained them in what to look for in hiring future leaders?

___ 6. Do you continually access their leadership skills and focus on the things they can do better? This must be done in a supportive and nurturing way!

___ 7. Do your leaders hire people who are more talented than the leader? If not, all you have are followers and little chance for dramatic growth.

John Schnatter, founder of Papa John's Pizza, was open minded enough to know that the true power of any organization is in its people. Continue to hire, train, and nurture leaders and you will one day be the best in your industry. Can you imagine your five or six employee company filled with men and women of vision and each year you hire one additional person with "leader math" mentality?

Keeping One Foot on First

Baudjuin once wrote, "To be ambitious for wealth, and yet always expecting to be poor; to be always doubting your ability to get what you long for, is like trying to reach east by traveling west. In sports terms: you can't steal second base by keeping one foot on first! There is not a person who does not long for success in some form, whether money, contentment, or fame. No matter how hard you work for success, your mind will stop your progress if you are occupied with thoughts of failure. These thoughts are fueled by the emotion of fear. It is one of the strangest of all emotions. Why? Because the things we fear seldom become reality! If you live in fear of something, it controls your life, but in an imaginary way! It is never the "thing" that controls us, but our own emotion.

Are you tired of not reaching your dreams? Are you tired of living in fear of public speaking, heights, or success? There is a formula to overcome your fear, whatever it might be.

1.   Study fear, and more specifically, the one fear that is holding you back. Isolate the few things about the fear that cause you anxiety. If it is public speaking, you might isolate the thoughts that you will forget your speech or that people will not like you.

2.   Write down why these things are not likely to happen and more specifically, the actions you can take to prevent them from happening. In the case of the speech, the actions of practicing and performing for a small group first would help insure you cannot fail.

3.   Make a list of the things you will feel and gain once you have

done the thing you fear. A newfound confidence, financial gain, self-esteem, and the joy of doing what you thought you could not, are all wonderful results of facing your fear.

4. Be intense! Make the decision to move forward with focus and determination.

5. Set a date to start. Create your own "D" Day: your "Dream" day when you will no longer be chained by your own fears! You will be liberated from fear and failure, moving to a higher level of personal success.

Everyone has the capacity to reach unlimited heights. The story of men and women is the story of common people doing uncommon things and the impossible becoming possible. The greatest barrier mankind has every faced is the personal barrier of the mind. Once broken, you can never go back to mediocrity! Break your chains to-day. Turn fear into fun, failure into success, and begin your new life, one that you control!

Don't Make New Year's Resolutions

WHAT? EVERYBODY MAKES New Year's resolutions! You know the ones. You plan to lose twenty pounds! You are going to work less and spend more time with family! You are going to start an investment account or buy real estate. The New Year comes and goes and within weeks, you are off your diet, working late, and wondering where all the money goes! Welcome to the world of good intentions with no plan of attack! If you want to make a New Year's resolution work, then stop making them!

No. That does not mean ignoring change or not setting goals. It means begin with a reasonable plan that is attainable on a daily and weekly basis.

Start with the goal you want to accomplish. Let's say it is losing ten pounds within a certain time frame. Write your goal on a 3X5 card in "results terms." An example would be, "On March 31, 2005, I weighed 145 lbs. which is ten pounds less than on January 1, 2005." Why future terms? Subconsciously, the brain interprets positive future statements as if they had already happened.

Your second step is to list all the positive benefits of losing ten pounds. This could be things like looking better, feeling better, or being healthier for those you love. We must always see positive benefits to everything we want to accomplish. We cannot expect to lose ten pounds if there is not a positive result that can be clearly stated. Every human being works from the focus of positive motivation. Once again, we have to repeat the positive benefits often in order to stay focused.

The third step is to make a list of actions that you are capable of performing on a regular basis, which will lead to your positive results. If you list going to the gym and you know you are likely to run out of time to make this commitment, do not list it. In fact, start your commitments in very small, workable timeframes. If you know you like to walk, then make one of your actions walking, but start with only ten minutes. As you develop the habit of walking you can extend your time. As far as eating, begin to eliminate small portions from your meals or slowly change your eating habits. The reason people fail at dieting is that they make such a dramatic shift in their eating habits and cannot sustain the change. It's too overwhelming and unattainable right off the bat. It's better to start small and gradually work your way up, than to start too high and give up.

One of the most important steps is to find a coach or accountability partner that will agree to review your goals with you on a weekly basis and help you stay on course. It is amazing what we will do when we know someone is watching. Coaching Tip: Do not make your coach your spouse or significant other! I think you know why!

Last but not least, reward yourself for your efforts—as well as results—and stay away from negative influences. That includes negative people who are well meaning but end up discouraging you. No one can rain on your parade if you do not let them!

This is not a complicated formula, but it does work! You can apply it to business, personal, family, investments, health, and your mental well-being! Start today, you will not be sorry!

Eternal Youth

LEGEND HAS IT that the Spanish explorer Juan Ponce de Leon searched for magic waters that could restore youth. Then, during his exploration, he discovered and named Florida. In the city of St. Augustine, Florida there is an actual tourist attraction for the "Fountain of Youth." The legend of Ponce de Leon's search has never been verified, but it makes an interesting story and a great question. Is eternal youth possible?

In one way, it is. There are some magical things in life that make us feel young. The greatest of these might be our dreams. Ralph Waldo Emerson said, "We need not count a man's years until he has nothing else to count." Emerson recognized that as long as we have something to live for, something that inspires us, we are never old in mind.

Some people are criticized as "dreamers." These are the people that have dreams, but never seem to move forward with those dreams. Anna Mary Robertson Moses (September 7, 1860 – December 13, 1961), better known as "Grandma Moses", was a renowned American folk artist. She is often cited as an example of an individual successfully beginning a career in the arts at an advanced age. Her family and friends called her either "Mother Moses" or "Grandma Moses", and although she first exhibited as "Mrs. Moses", the press eagerly dubbed her "Grandma Moses", which stuck. LIFE magazine celebrated her 100th birthday by featuring her on its September 19, 1960 cover. She did not start painting until her seventies and finished over 1600 canvases. Old in body, yes, but young at heart. She fulfilled a life-long dream.

People who stay young at heart never think about death or growing old, their minds are filled with dreams and action. Ever wonder why so many people retire and often pass away within months? Too much time with no dreams. People who stay young at heart spend their time laughing and refuse to waste time with anger or envy. They fill their time with ideas, activities, and dreams. They don't just breathe. They live.

Nola Hills Ochs became the oldest college graduate in the world at 95 years old, graduating from Fort Hays State University in 2007. In 2010, at 98 years old she earned her Master's Degree. By the way, her undergraduate degree record was broken by a 96-year-old gentleman from Taiwan! Go Nola! Young at heart? Absolutely!

Oldest Olympic gold medalist? That honor goes to Joshua Millner of Great Britain who won a gold medal in free rifle, 1000 yards, at the young age of 61.

These stories are endless and inspiring. Your dreams are your "fountain of youth," provided that you begin to take action toward your dreams. You are as young as your dreams and as old as your doubts. One step toward your dream will lead to another until you stand upon the victory stand of life. Live to laugh, live to learn, but most of all, live to win!

Victim of Circumstance?

IS THIS YOUR day or week? You have another deadline to meet and you say, "I hate this stress. I want a less stressful job!" You get home and the kids are driving you crazy. Your best friend wants to borrow money and you resent the fact he or she has never paid you back the last time. You got cut off in traffic and your stress level went through the roof. Late at night you wonder, "How did life become so complicated and stressful? Why me?" The next week, your boss praises you for a job well done, your spouse tells you how wonderful you are, you get a great job offer from a competitor, and you think, "Isn't life great!" The cycle continues...life is a series of fortunate and unfortunate events. What is really amazing is how we allow these events to turn us into victims. How can we be happy and content one minute and then stressed and miserable the next? Here is the lesson we all need to learn.

We are the makers and shapers of our own destiny. To truly begin enjoying what life offers us on a consistent basis, a person, at some point in life, must change the way he or she interprets events. Unfortunate things will always enter life at the least expected times. It is our reaction and interpretation that gives these events their life, whether good or bad. How often does a seemingly bad or tragic event lead to unexpected success? We all have stories to tell about success coming from tragedy. You will always be on a roller coaster of emotional ups and downs until you realize that the power of your thinking and the transformation of these thoughts into positive action can make the worst event your shining triumph! The next time life deals you an empty hand, rather than be a prisoner to negative emotion and stress, follow this life changing strategy:

1. Focus your thoughts not on the event itself, but on your options.

2. Choose options that will lead you out of the darkness of self-pity and stress the fastest!

3. Take immediate action. It might mean simply calling a friend for support or taking one small baby step to recovery.

4. When the negative thinking creeps back in, throw yourself back into focused, unrelenting action. Instead of lying in bed feeling sorry for yourself, get up! Even if it is 3 o'clock in the morning...take action!

5. Evaluate your course after doing this several times and decide if it is working. If it's not, take a new path; but do not quit!

Human beings are so amazing! Within the power of our own thoughts lies the key to happiness and riches. Start "Minding" for goal today. You are the most extraordinary human being ever created! There is no one like you...Live to Win!

The Rocket Boys

ON A STARRY October night in 1957, a fourteen-year old boy in Coalwood, West Virginia looked into the wonder of space and saw the first satellite, the Russian Sputnik, streak across the lonely sky. At that moment, he realized his dream. He wanted to be a rocket scientist. His dream, once planted, would not leave, but grew into the dream of a small coal-mining town. Homer Hickam Jr. gathered a small group of teenage boys together and began building rockets in the basement of his home. They were the laughing stock of the town, where young men did not escape the mines. They dreamed of scholarships and futures far brighter than the October sky. Against all odds, they ventured forth in their quest, inspired by their chemistry teacher, Freida Riley.

Boys from Coalwood never went to college, with the exception of those earning a football scholarship. Ms. Riley inspired the group of boys to enter the county science fair with hopes of going to the nationals and gaining recognition that would enable them to reach their dreams. Against all odds, they succeeded and won the national science fair in 1960. They became known as "The Rocket Boys," and they all went to college. Homer Hickam Jr. became a NASA scientist as he had predicted. Their story is told in the hit movie "October Sky" and Hickam's book, The Rocket Boys.

The secret ingredients to reaching your dreams are hidden in this inspiring story.

1. Develop a wondrous passion for what you want out of life. A life

filled with passion is a truly joyful life.

2. Surround yourself with positive mentors, as the Rocket Boys did with Ms. Riley. While it is necessary that you believe in yourself, it is also very important to have others who support and believe in you, because the road to your dreams will be lonely and perilous at times.

3. Embrace failure as your friend. The Rocket Boys faced constant failure and were discouraged, but they learned from each failure and grew in spirit and wisdom.

4. Walk daily in the direction of your dreams. It takes a thousand small steps to climb the mountain of success. It never comes in giant, easy leaps. No day can go by that you do not take one action step.

5. Never stop dreaming. When you stop dreaming, you stop hoping. A life without hope is an empty one indeed. At that point in life, we merely exist, settling for the leftovers that life throws our way.

As a leader, never stop believing that all things are possible. How can you inspire those that work for you if they see you without vision, passion, and belief? How can you hope to surpass your goals and objectives without a burning desire to reach for the stars? You do not have to be a great speaker or have a dynamic personality to accomplish this. You only need to be a leader by example. Walk the walk and others will follow you to the stars!

Live Like You Were Dying

I WAS SCANNING through the radio stations on a long drive when a country song hit me. Maybe it was fate, but the words caught my ears like a siren. The song was "Live Like You Were Dying" by Tim McGraw. In the song he is talking to a friend who received bad news from his doctor. He found out that he was terminally ill. When he asks the friend, "What did you do?" it starts the chorus of the song…

"I went sky divin'
I went Rocky Mountain climbin'
I went 2.7 seconds on a bull named Fu Manchu.
And I loved a little deeper
And I spoke a little sweeter
And I gave forgiveness I'd been denyin'

And I hope someday you get the chance to live like you were dyin'."
Have you ever sat in contemplation of your life? I began to review this year and past year's and asked myself that question, "Have I lived life to its fullest and best?" My honest reply was "No." Sure, we have goals but they are more dreams than goals. We think about them and wish for them, but seldom put together a plan to achieve them. As sales professionals we can live our professional life to the fullest by being excited when we are with clients and making sure they have the best experience possible.

As mothers and fathers, sons and daughters, we can put our best into relationships by giving our best to our loved ones through patience, kind and thoughtful words, and simply our precious time. Make every hour count! Make every minute a treasure! One smile from a child's lovely face is worth all the closings in the world! A hug and a kiss is a lifetime of memories compressed into a moment of wonder! Guys, go get a card for your special someone and mail it today. Tell her how much you treasure her. Ladies, have a hug and kiss ready when you first see each other at the end of the day!

Living life like you were dying means more than excitement. It means reaching out and grabbing for everything you ever thought was important, from your son's high school football game to singing a little one to sleep each night. It means dreaming together and working with passion to make the dreams come true. I was once told that to laugh, and sing, to hope and to dream, to love each day for the wonder each day holds is nothing more than a choice freely made and with no regrets, with no hatred, with no resentment. Letting go of the negative fills your life with the positives, but most of all .... hope for a wonderful life!

"I was finally the husband most of the time I wasn't
I became a friend a friend would like to have.
All of a sudden goin' fishin' wasn't an imposition,
I went three times the year I lost my dad.
Well I finally read the Good Book
and I took a good long hard look
At what I'd do if I could do it all again."
And I hope that someday you'll get the chance...
To live like you were dyin'."

If I Could See

HELEN KELLER, ALTHOUGH blind and deaf, never stopped achieving during her lifetime. There were no limits to the things she wanted to accomplish. Once a reporter asked her, "How difficult is it being blind?" Her reply was, "Not as difficult as having sight, but having no vision!" Vision is that wondrous ability to see what others cannot; to see the possibilities that exist in both tragedy and opportunity. Vision is not a talent or even a gift. It is a way of thinking; a state of mind. Vision is believing in the possibilities that exist in life!

What happens to keep us from having the vision to create our own destiny? In one short word: life. We become so caught up in just getting through the day that the average person stops thinking about the endless possibilities within his or her reach. It is not difficult to start thinking with vision again since everyone at some time has possessed this wonderful power!

It starts with believing that you deserve abundance. The dictionary definition of abundance is "ample sufficiency," meaning all that we need. An abundant life is one that is filled with the important things, loved ones, a fulfilling career, and high values. As our vision relates to these important things, we can start dreaming of the life we deserve. The second step is to know what is most important to us and use it as a motivator to take action.

Taking action on anything is fueled by a passionate desire. You cannot have vision or make change unless you want something with all of your heart. Cal Ripkin, the ironman of baseball, who played more consecutive games than anyone in major league history, always had a passion for baseball from the time he was a small boy. He lived and breathed the game and attributed his success to desire over talent. Take action every day until you achieve your destiny!

Will it be easy? No. Nothing worthwhile is ever easy! One of the greatest truths and greatest secrets of success is this: life gives its most wondrous treasures to those who never stop trying, to whom failure is temporary and success is just an effort away. Obstacles are welcome; they serve to strengthen the resolve of winners. This is based on a mindset, not talent.

As Helen Keller expressed, it is far worse to have no vision than it is to be physically blind. When you cannot see the dreams that are before you, life loses its boundless joy, days turn into the grind of weeks, months, and years and in the end, we can only wonder what the possibilities may have been. Dream great dreams. See the possibilities in your life! You have no limits.

The Greatest Law of the Universe

I KNOW YOU have done this. You are looking for a parking space in a crowded mall and you start visualizing a space near the front. Suddenly, a car pulls out on the front row! You are preparing for a big business presentation and you believe with your heart and soul that it is a dynamic event and you will be inspiring! Guess what? It happens! I remember preparing for my very first motivational talk in front of a large real estate group. I took a long walk on the beach the day before and visualized a standing ovation! Guess what? It happened just as I had visualized it! All of these things represent one of the greatest laws of the universe: the law of attraction!

We attract into our lives the very same thing we believe in our subconscious will appear. Our mental and emotional state attracts into our lives the same emotional state. If you are filled with anxiety and despair, these things will most likely enter your life. Why? The law of attraction! The rules are very clear.

- A negative emotion, in most cases, gives off a feeling to others. If I believe I will lose the sale, the prospect picks up on my doubt and becomes nervous or unsure.

- Negative thoughts not only create more negative thoughts, they attract negative actions and feelings from others.

- If I believe there is no business or that all "customers" are tough to deal with, I will attract those kinds of people.

- If I believe every consumer is only concerned about price,

price will always be a major issue and I will always be competing on price.

- On the positive side the rules state:

- If I believe that great things will happen, I bring into my life the forces that will create this, provided I pay the price of hard work.

- The positive emotions I give off to others are like magnets that attract people into my life. I have a friend in Dallas, Texas named Skip Johnson. Within ten minutes of entering a room, he creates an incredible amount of positive energy that attracts everyone to him, even though he is a very humble individual!

- If I have an excitement for my company, my profession, and my clients, those emotions spread and before long I have plenty of clients!

- If I visualize all the dreams that I want to attract into my life, they will come to me over time provided I truly believe and take the necessary actions to create the dreams!

Confidence is the key ingredient in the law of attraction; the true belief in events, in dreams, and in ones self. George Herbert wrote, "Skill and confidence are an unconquerable army!" Ever wonder why some people have that magic quality called "charisma?" It is because their thoughts, their passions, and their beliefs broadcast out like a search light in the dark, attracting all ships in the harbor. The negative among us will discount the law of attraction, saying it is motivational hype. Those who have experienced its power will quietly sit back and smile. They know the real truth!

What Life Have You Touched Today?

IT WAS HIS birthday. Like any ten-year-old boy, he was excited! At a party given by his relatives, he received many small gifts, but anticipated most the gift he was going to receive from his mother. He was hurt when she announced that she did not have a gift, but that she did have a surprise for him on the next day.

Early the next morning, she took him to the family car as she carried two paper bags, one with his toys and the other with his clothes. After a drive of several hours, they arrived at what looked like a ranch far out in rural Alabama. She led him to the front door of a wooden house, knocked, and a giant of a man appeared. The mother announced that she no longer wanted the little boy and he would now be living at the ranch. The broken-hearted ten-year-old cried as she drove away, never to return. The 6'6" man lifted little Keith Denton up and told him four things: "I love you," "I will never leave you," "You will always have a home," and "Don't ever lie to me, or I'll know." Welcome to the Big Oak Ranch for boys sponsored by Paul Bear Bryant, the great coach at the University of Alabama, and run by one of his former players.

Before going to Big Oak Ranch, Keith was a troublemaker in school and even stole money from the teachers at his elementary school while they were at faculty meetings. Keith continued his rebellious and troublemaking ways at the ranch, but this time, as promised, no one stopped loving or caring for him. Keith went on to graduate as the valedictorian of his high school class, was All State in football, and received academic scholarship offers to Princeton, Harvard, and

West Point! His dramatic transformation can be summed up in one word. Love.

Every human wants to know that someone cares, whether an adult or a child, employee or student, husband or wife. What have you done today to touch a life? Sometimes it is as simple as showing patience. Sometimes it is just taking the time to say how much you care. It is not difficult to touch the lives of others if we simply focus on "random acts of kindness." Let a co-worker know how much you appreciate him or her. Tell your spouse how important he or she is and how much you truly care. Ask your children about their day and tell them how proud you are of what they do. The wonderful thing about touching lives is how deeply it touches us in return. If you are like most Americans, you live from day-to-day, just doing your job. Each of us is at our best when we give to others. Take the time to get involved with those who need to know you care, whether it is little league or the local homeless shelter.

What about Keith Denton? Well, he wanted to be a lawyer and graduated from law school, but he was called to touch lives in a different way. He returned to Big Oak with his wife and started a development campaign to raise funds and in four years, raised over 15 million dollars! Today he has started another home for abused girls in Jacksonville, Florida. And the cycle of love goes on to eternity. Touch someone today and you will be rewarded a thousand times over!

Dangerous Words

DO YOU BELIEVE in self-talk? Do you believe that the words you speak to yourself can impact your daily life and ultimately your success? There is little debate over the fact that thoughts shape our daily actions and ultimately our lives. William Shakespeare wrote, "There is nothing either good or bad, but thinking makes it so." If he was right, then thinking can truly change our world if we understand how to "think right."

Thinking right involves choosing our internal words carefully. If a person makes a mistake, often he or she will be tougher on himself or herself than anyone else. In fact, we often carry the mistake forward into other tasks and situations creating a multiplier effect! The more we think negative thoughts internally, the more they will become self-fulfilling prophesies. The words we speak to ourselves can be the most uplifting or the most devastating. Your thoughts forge a chain of events that, if left unchecked, can emerge as triumph or disaster. What is the chain of events that can change our life?

- Thoughts, whether good or bad, lead to ideas. The ideas are usually verbalized or stored into the unconscious mind. These ideas are either rationalized ("not my fault!") or begin to grow into a power. That power is belief. Begin to believe your thoughts and ideas; you begin a journey of success or failure.

- Ideas are born from thought. Ideas have both changed the world for the best and destroyed it.

- Ideas put into action lead to results of some kind, not always the ones we want or expect, but results just the same. The action should be consistent with our true belief system or we will fail!

- Actions repeated often enough become a very powerful thing: habit. The world is built on habit. Habits can make us powerful or lead to a path of destruction. Take exercise as an example. When we first start, we are excited about getting in shape and looking good. If we have a plan on how we are going to get in shape and then workout on a consistent basis, guess what? We build a great body, improve health, and become stronger! If we do not convert our thoughts into actions, repeat them until they become habit, nothing changes.

- Solid, positive habits lead us to the creation of personal destiny. Many people think that destiny is something that cannot be controlled. In reality, we shape our own destiny. Thoughts lead to ideas, ideas lead to actions, consistent actions lead to habits, and habits lead to destiny. We are truly the makers and shapers of the life we currently live. If you wish to change your life, change your thoughts!

James Allen, noted American Psychologist, wrote, "Our life is what our thoughts make it. A man will find that as he alters his thoughts toward things and other people, things and other people will alter towards him." You will always become your thoughts. Make them positive. Make them powerful. Most of all, make them worthy!

Mirrors or Windows?

WHAT DO YOU see when you look into a mirror? Yourself, of course! While it is important to "know ourselves," it is also important to look beyond the mirror. Think of life as one of either mirrors or windows. A life of mirrors is one that contains limitations. We seldom see beyond our current life or situation. Each day begins to look the same as the one that just ended. Ralph Waldo Emerson wrote, "Most men live lives of quiet desperation." What he meant is that most people simply endure life. If your life is filled with mirrors, then you will never see beyond yourself and your present situation. Imagine a different viewpoint, a life filled with windows.

When you look out of a window, the possibilities are endless! There are a thousand small details as well as the distant horizon of sky, clouds, stars, the sun, and moon. Look at a window as the opportunity not only to gain a new perspective beyond yourself, but also to discover new possibilities in your life. Remember when you were in high school and you wanted to go to the dance with that "special" person? You probably practiced what you were going to say in front of the mirror, but never got beyond the mirror to actually ask the person or let his or her friend know you had an interest. Looking through a window, you could have imagined all of the possibilities and positives that existed on the other side, maybe even a "yes!" How can you begin living a life filled with windows and fewer mirrors?

The first step is to stop selling yourself short. You must believe in the possibilities beyond the window. A world is waiting for your passion, belief, and ideas! You are the first barrier. Overcome this important obstacle, and you have accomplished the most difficult part of the task.

The second step is to stop limiting your thinking. Every idea has the potential to expand to meet the size of your beliefs and expectations. When Bill Gates, founder of Microsoft, signed his first contract to deliver an operating system to IBM, he did not have a product yet! His team worked twenty-four hours a day, seven days a week and delivered MS-DOS to the computer giant. Bill Gates said he never doubted for a moment that he would not succeed.

The final step is to never stop improving the view. Just as we add a garden to our landscape to improve the view, we are not limited to merely looking through the window. We can walk outside and improve our perspective and our world. Never believe for a moment that you cannot change the environment around you. Men and women throughout history have changed the course of the world through gaining a new perspective beyond the mirrors of themselves to the endless possibilities beyond the horizon. Look out of your window and see the stars!

Lessons from Geese

IT IS THAT time of year when birds begin migrating to their winter homes. One of the most remarkable of the migrating birds is the goose. As geese silhouette the autumn sky, their distinctive "V" formation is always inspiring. It serves a very real purpose and could even stand for "values." Yes, even the animal kingdom operates from a set of principals for living.

1. As geese fly in a "V" formation, each goose behind the leader has less wind resistance so that the entire group can fly more than 71% further than if they did not. Geese work as a team to create success. It would not be possible to reach their destination in time for winter if they did not share the workload and sacrifice for the good of the team.

2. They take turns leading and sharing the workload. There is no "ego." Each goose takes the responsibility of leadership and the extra effort that accompanies the task. It is hard to imagine one goose complaining about responsibility or taking the lead! Each one, in turn, takes the responsibility.

3. If one goose is wounded or falls out of formation, two geese will follow and stay with it until it either dies or recovers. Then, they will join another flock and continue the journey. Loyalty and care exist within the team.

4. The geese flying in formation "honk" at each other to encourage the group to continue making a supreme effort. Encouraging each other in the team helps us reach heights we never imagined. Let's

make sure our "honking" is always encouraging and inspiring, not negative.

The lessons here are clear:

As people (or geese) work together, forget ego and selfish interests, and begin thinking less about "I" and more in terms of what we can all accomplish working together as team, nothing is impossible.

The great inventor, Thomas Edison, had many people working with him, mostly young and aspiring inventors. He accomplished so much and held more patents than anyone in the world, because his team always came before himself. He encouraged the young scientists under him and gave them full credit for their accomplishments. Not only was he a great inventor, but he was a great coach, mentor, and leader as well. When you get the chance to become the "lead goose," never forget all of the geese behind you. You cannot do it alone!

The most important lesson of all is universal; as we strive to help our fellow man, as we stand up to make a difference, the effect is multiplied and miracles begin to take place in the lives of people and in our communities. Nothing is out of the grasp of those who have the courage and passion to be a true leader.

Taking Poison

I RECENTLY SPOKE with an old friend who was angry about a situation that he could not control. The more he spoke about the situation, the angrier he became, until it seemed like he was possessed. Days later, he was still complaining and worrying. As I continued to listen, a thought began to process through my brain, "How many people waste their productive energy being angry or worrying over what they cannot control?" There is an old Chinese proverb that says, "If you are patient in one moment of anger, you will escape a hundred days of sorrow." All things in life are based on choices. You really do choose to be angry. Think for a moment about this simple but true thought. "Being angry toward someone or worrying is like taking poison and waiting for someone else to die!"

Countering the effects of anger and worry can pay dramatic dividends if you have a plan for dealing with these negative and destructive emotions. The first step in your plan is the power of reasoning. If you were to reason during any volatile situation, you would probably conclude the following:

- Do you have enough information to determine how you can remedy this situation? Often, just a little soul searching can lead you to a more realistic view of your part in the problem.

- Do you have the ability to control this situation? If you do not, let it go and spend your time in some productive task.

- What will you gain personally through worry and anger? You know the answer to that question: nothing. In fact, you will create monumental stress in your life.

- Is there an action you can take now, this minute that will improve the situation? Usually, talking to the person or source of your anger in a constructive way can lead to a positive result.

- Always take the high road! No one ever lost who showed class, character, and dignity. Be the ultimate professional.

My angry friend was going to abandon the project that made him so angry. Instead, I convinced him to simply state his case with the client, reason out with them his expectations, and ask for alternatives. The company actually apologized and changed his contract to reflect his expectations. The light bulb went off! All that worry and frustration was for nothing. The writer Thomas Fuller said, "Act nothing in furious passion. It's like putting to sea in an angry storm." Here's wishing you calm seas and smooth sailing! Create your own "Special Day!"

Adversity Creates Power!

THE STORIES ARE endless and classic. We love to read about the person or group that, against all odds, beat the obstacles! Thomas Edison lost his hearing as a young boy, but never let it affect his thirst for knowledge and his passion for inventing. Albert Einstein was considered a slow learner and teachers encouraged him to quit school. Christopher Columbus was laughed at and ridiculed when he believed there was a western route to the East Indies; after all everyone knew the world was flat!

Unfortunately, most of us react to adversity by either giving up or simply enduring the event until it goes away. There is no life that does not face difficulties, many far worse than you will ever experience. How is it that some people can turn adversity into triumph while most of us allow it to control our destiny? Fortunately, the answer to this question is a simple one, yet few comprehend how to put the answer into action. It is all in the way a person thinks. Some men and women are naturally negative thinkers either by influence or by choice. It is those who make a conscious choice to fight and win that turn the worst situation into a marvelous success. This is a choice, not a gift or talent.

Victor Frankl wrote about his tragic experiences in a Nazi concentration camp in his famous book, Man's Search for Meaning. He saw hopelessness firsthand; he was starved, beaten, and separated from his family. Many gave up and died while others kept hope and their belief that they would survive. Dr. Frankl decided, while still in the camp, that he would use his experience to write a book about man's ability to show the positive side of humanity in the worst conditions.

The most powerful statement in his book was this: "When all things are taken away, there is always one thing that cannot be taken, man's ability to choose his attitude in any given circumstance." This single choice allowed men to either die or survive.

It is no different with our lives. Choosing to remain positive in the worst of circumstances will create more options and more solutions than we can ever imagine. Most breakthroughs in business and medicine were possible due to obstacles, disease, or other insurmountable barriers. Problems create opportunities for solutions! Think of it this way, if there are no problems, there are no solutions and no advancements to the next level.

Try this. When you face your next problem, immediately envision how a solution will not only solve the problem, but create a new opportunity for you to achieve great things. Create a list of possible solutions, decide which solution will get the best result, and take action. James Bilkey said it best, "You will never be the person you can be if pressure, tension, and discipline are taken out of your life." Face adversity with power, determination, and the will to win, and you will win!

Attitude is a Choice

OUR NATION EXPERIENCED a tragedy like no other in our history when 9/11 occurred. It has been a time of reflection. Many of us have begun to question not only the perilous times we live in, but also the true meaning of what we value most. This thought process combined with the uncertainty of the future, layoffs, and a stumbling economy have caused many to begin to doubt their place in life and to even become depressed. There is always triumph from every tragedy, but the victory is won through focus and action. It is a time of resolve. The forceful and dynamic choices we make at this point in our life become the measure of our character and our unshakable strength. What can you do now to rise above the chaos and uncertainty?

- Believe in our system. It creates opportunities for those willing to believe that all things are possible.

- Remember, time is the most powerful healer ever created. But, we only heal when we move forward with pride and courage.

- Believe in the power of one person: you. Not only to change your life, but the lives of everyone you touch as well. Live each day with the fullness and joy with which you have been blessed.

- Remember that no great things are accomplished without an undying passion and enthusiasm for life and for each day.

- Believe in your faith, whatever forms it may take. A great power guides this country and each person with a never-ending belief in justice, love, and a greater power than our own.

- Remember what is most important in your life and begin living according to those values. When you are not following your values, life becomes unbalanced and chaotic. Restore the calm by being at peace with your life's priorities.

- Believe in the power of this nation to overcome all adversity. There are few places on this earth that allow for the personal freedom, opportunity, and protection of our great nation of the people, by the people, and for the people.

Go home tonight, read to your children, and watch them as they slumber. Spend time in deep conversation with the special person in your life. Call a close friend or relative who you have not spoken to for a while. Most of all, take time to count the blessings in your life as you prepare to make life's most important choice; to choose your own attitude toward life and the personal power you possess to change your life.

How Could I Be So Lucky?

"HE'S ALWAYS SO lucky" could be the most often repeated phrase in the English language, maybe in any language! You know those people, the ones who have all the luck. They buy a raffle ticket and they win! They enter a contest and sure enough, they win again! In sales, they are always in the right place at the right time. They are so lucky! They always land the big deal! So, what is the mystery? What do "the lucky ones" do that the rest of us are missing?

The fact that we are willing to believe that luck is a major factor in anyone's success is to excuse ourselves from success. Sure, when someone buys a lottery ticket and wins, you could classify that as luck, but in reality it is only random chance however remote the chances of winning might be. It is true that some people seem to be assisted by luck more than others, but if you truly evaluate the characteristics of the lucky person you can begin to make sense of the concept of luck.

First, lucky people expect to win. They expect good things to happen. It is almost a "law of attraction." Their very attitude attracts positive things. This is not mystical, but it is logical. If you expect good things to happen you tend to become more positive and, in turn, affect people in a positive way. When you are positive with people they want to work with you, help you, and even buy from you! Wait. What about that lottery ticket? Random chance!

Second, lucky people, because they feel lucky, seem to be more active in creating their own "destiny." Not only do they act more positive, they take more positive actions. They meet more people, talk to more people, and spread a feeling of positive emotion. You could say lucky people take more positive action because they believe good things will happen!

Lucky people are usually willing to help others. They thrive on spreading cheerfulness, joy, and excitement. People love to be around "lucky people." Why? They make us feel good and they make us feel lucky! Somehow we believe their luck will "rub off" on us, and you know what? In many cases, it does! I know, you are still thinking about the lottery ticket. Trust me, random chance!

Lucky people take action! They are participants in the game of life. Unlucky things happen to them, but they move on and choose to take action, rather than drown in their own sorrow. Have you ever seen an unhappy person who is lucky? I did not think so. Luck is that wonderful thing that happens when an industrious, hard working person runs into an opportunity that his or her hard work made the person prepared to take advantage of the situation!

I know what you are thinking! "Ken, there has to be more to this luck thing!" Give it up! Stop excusing away the true essence of luck, put best by Max O'Rell: "Luck means the hardships and privations which you have not hesitated to endure, the long nights you have devoted to work. Luck means the appointments you have never failed to keep; the trains you have never failed to catch." Hey, go buy a lottery ticket, and when you do, act like you are going to win! Who knows? Live to laugh, live to love, and live to win!

Change This, Change Your World

THERE IS A single word that best describes all the failed marriages, mediocre careers, broken friendships, and miserable people. That word is "attitude." A great test to determine your own attitude is to ask yourself this question, "How is life treating you?" If the answer is, "Terrible," then, in most cases, it is a reflection of your attitude. Change your attitude, change your world! It is at this point you are saying, "Easier said than done." The truth is, your attitude can change by performing a single action, making one choice. The power of choice is always within our reach. Wilma Askinas said, "There is no better measure of a person, than what he does when he is absolutely free to choose."

There is a "formula" to choosing well. It is not complicated and does not require any special skills or talents. Follow the formula and your choices are great ones. Do not follow the formula and your decisions do not always have the best results.

Step One: When you make decisions, ask yourself, "Will this choice help me be a better person or help those that are most important to me?" It is hard to make a bad choice based on this thinking. This question often creates the toughest choices, however. For instance, choosing to get a higher education comes at great sacrifice and in the short term may create financial hardship and a loss of short-term freedom. A choice to pursue a dream can mean the chance of failure.

Step Two: Think your choice out step-by-step. Major decisions can seem overwhelming and even depressing. When broken down into steps that can be performed more easily, we are more likely to not only make the difficult choice, but to follow that choice. If you decide to go on a diet, break your eating plan down into single days, choose the best foods for you, and decide to keep a journal. Now you have more substance to your choice and a step-by-step plan for success.

Three: Take action on your choice immediately. Nothing in this world builds self-esteem like taking positive action. After making a decision, every day that you wait dramatically diminishes the chances you will succeed. The trait of all great leaders is this: they are decisive. The best leaders know the power of decisiveness for it creates resolve and focus. It sends a message to others of the power to accomplish a given task.

Finally, if you truly believe in your decision, do not falter when obstacles arise. Be resolved to stay the course no matter what may happen. Greatness comes from an unfaltering vision and determination to succeed at our choices. Choose well, formulate your plan step- by-step, take unrelenting action and only one attitude can emerge, one of courage and positive thinking. The great author, Thornton Wilder said, "The more decisions you are forced to make alone, the more you are aware of your freedom to choose." Choose today, but choose greatness, there is power in great choices and great dreams!

How to Motivate Others

"I DON'T UNDERSTAND. I work hard at motivating my sales force and it seems like a never-ending battle! The more I do for them the more they expect from me!" This is the typical response of a sales manager or operations manager when discussing the "M" word. Why does it seem so difficult to motivate people to do a great job? The answer is not obvious and is often the opposite of what we think.

Motivation literally means "to move forward." The mistake we make is thinking that we can actually do the moving as managers or leaders. People can only motivate themselves. Even when they tell us, "You really motivated me to work harder," in reality, they made an internal decision that what they were doing was not effective and it was time to change. As the leader, you provided an environment for change. To do this, you need to be aware of some basic facts about motivation.

First, we have to look at what de-motivates people in order to figure out how to allow them to motivate themselves. There are two primary de-motivators in a working environment. The most powerful of the workplace de-motivators is "organizational obstacles." An organizational obstacle is defined as an impediment that exists within the company making it difficult for us to do our job. Sometimes these obstacles exist for a reason, but most often it is the wrong reason. For example, a department store has a problem with a high number of returned items. To solve the problem, management decides to only give credits for purchases on refunds, but no cash back. In their mind, this will protect their profit margin because the consumer will still have to buy another item from their store. In reality, the front line employees have to deal with a large number of angry customers who want their money back! The customers grudgingly accept their credit slips but vow never to come back to the store, and the front line employees are stressed, de-motivated, and have a loss in respect for management. Net result? Fewer customers, higher turnover, and monetary loss. This decision becomes an organizational obstacle.

Identifying organizational obstacles is simple. You ask employees, "What obstacles make it more difficult to do your job and serve your customer?" That is the easy part. The more difficult part is actually having the leadership courage to make the change. Once you decide to make the change, let the employees decide how to do so and be responsible for change. If you do not, you are doomed for failure.

The second biggest de-motivator is you: the leader! This does not mean that you are not positive or sensitive to the needs of your people. It usually means that you are not allowing them to take possession or ownership of their job. No matter how kind you are to your employees, if they do not feel they have a part in their own destiny, they will quickly become de-motivated. The leader says, "I'm always positive and take time to recognize my people! I don't understand why they are not motivated?" It is like telling teenagers how great they did in their drivers' education class, but you still will not let them drive the family car. What is the unspoken message? I do not trust you, and I do not think you are good enough. A great leader gives ownership to the people. Even when they come to the leader with a problem, he or she does not solve the problem, but guides the employees to solve their own problem. By doing this, you have boosted their self-esteem and their worth to you. They have become a more valuable asset.

How do you tell if you are the non-empowering leader? Sign number one: you are constantly putting out fires. You are the hero that comes to the rescue. Great satisfaction is gained by you, the employees dump more problems on you and they take no ownership. The second sign is the same mistakes occur repeatedly. Once again, you have told them what to do, but why do not they do it? Because they have no ownership!

How do you motivate people for long-term results? Remove organizational obstacles and become a leader that empowers people to solve their own problems. After you do these things, reward, recognize, and party to your heart's content! Are we having fun yet?

Making the Best of Life

JOHN WOODEN, THE great UCLA basketball coach who won more NCAA championships than any collegiate coach in history, once made a profound statement about life in general. He said, "Things turn out best for the people who make the best of the way things turn out!" I think he was talking about the most powerful determiner of success: attitude. Attitude is a choice, not an emotion, not a talent that some possess and others do not, not a complicated skill to be learned, but a choice. It can be a difficult choice, especially in the face of adversity or tragedy, yet there are those among us who are still able to make the right choice.

Think of attitude as a discipline, the same as staying fit or keeping up to date in a profession. You must work at it daily in order to make it work for you. I think the best description of attitude is "doing what builds our character and our life to the highest degree." The natural result of attitude is action. A great attitude produces an abundance of positive action. A poor attitude creates no action or destructive behavior. Procrastination is the result of a poor attitude. The way we treat people is a result of poor attitude. The interesting thing is this: it all starts and forms in our daily thoughts.

Thinking is like getting in shape. The more positive and productive thoughts we have, the more success we realize. Earnest Henley's great poem "Invictus" is the ultimate reflection of the power of thought and attitude. The last four lines of the poem say it all.

"It matters not how straight the gate,

How charged with punishments the scroll,

I am the master of my fate

I am the captain of my soul!"

"Invictus" is an autobiographical poem. Henley had an incredibly turbulent life. He was one of six children raised in poverty. He was afflicted with tubercular arthritis at age 12. His left leg was amputated when he was 16. He spent months in hospitals struggling with illness and he lost his only child to cerebral meningitis. Yet, he was one of England's most celebrated poets and playwrights. The author was writing from personal experience and his life is a tribute to maintaining a great attitude in the face of constant adversity.

Today is a wonderful opportunity. It affords you the chance in a single moment of time to alter the course of your history, to change the direction of your life, to make a difference. The special moment comes when you make the choice, when you choose to be among the conquerors of life, not the vanquished, when you refuse to let the occurrences of each day determine your outlook like the ebb and flow of the tides. From your first thought when you awake at sunrise, until the last thought at midnight, choose to be a positive participant in the game of life and you will be one of life's "All Stars."

The Buck Stops Here!

PRESIDENT HARRY S. Truman was known as a no-nonsense, straightforward man. His slogan was "The buck stops here!" As President of the United States, he believed he was responsible for what happened during his presidency and once he acted, he stood by his decisions. He made what was possibly one of the most difficult decisions that one man has ever made in the history of the world; the decision to drop the atomic bomb. He was criticized and condemned worldwide, but his interest was clear, saving what was estimated to be the potential death of over 200,000 more American servicemen if the war was taken to the shores of Japan. Truman never apologized for his decision and he took 100% responsibility.

When you examine your life carefully, you will find it is the sum total of the decisions you have made, and even more important, the ones you failed to make. The ebb and flow of life is based on these choices, these decisions. When decisions are made, too often people do not take the approach of Harry Truman. Instead of taking full responsibility, it is often "someone or something else's fault." You choose a job that you do not like and it's your boss's fault. You drop out of college and your lack of education holds you back. None of these things are the real reason for any limitations created in life, you are the reason! The moment you choose to not take responsibility for your choices and your actions you give up your right to move forward in life. You see, excuses allow you to stop fighting, to stop achieving, and blame the world, circumstances, or others for your own personal failures. Taking responsibility allows you to move forward with your head held high, to learn, to grow, to become what you were intended to be, a champion.

In the book The Traveler's Gift by Andy Andrews, he writes, "My life will be a statement, not an apology." He also wrote, "I will not have a problem to deal with, but a choice to make." I think one of the greatest decisions a human being can make is the decision to accept full responsibility for his or her life, to escape the bonds of excuses, failure, and "poor me," and make the decision to become the master of fate, not the victim. There is an incredible feeling of power when you are released from the prison of excuses and embrace your destiny! From that moment you are free to pursue your destiny by breaking the shackles of "poor me," and you reach for all you can be, life takes a different direction, one filled with great choices!

It's time! It's time to claim what is yours! Everyone has greatness within, the chance to create, to live life to its fullest. Success is measured in so many different ways. Maybe the ultimate success is simply living each day with purpose, with the full measure of heart and passion, no matter the failures, the setbacks. The great thing about the path of life is this, "Whether in dark of night or the light of day, whether storm or calm, we can create and control our ability to smile, to laugh, to hope and to dream. Never give up your choices. You are responsible for your life!"

The Greatest Gift

EVERY NATION HAS special times of year, when there is a spirit of giving and a spirit of remembrance. The exchange of gifts, family gatherings, and special ceremonies all mark events that fill human beings with a feeling of giving. You can give many things for many reasons. Physical gifts to friends and loved ones, gifts of money and time to charities, spending time with those less fortunate are all acts of kindness. They mean little, however, unless we give what is most important: our hearts!

When I speak of "heart" it means the inner self of every human being who wants to make a difference, who wants to touch a life in a positive way. Here is to each of you who gives from the heart!

- To the firefighter who enters the burning building one more time and risks his or her life for another.

- To the national guardsmen who leaves family and friends to help in disaster torn regions of the world and disaster at home.

- To the mortgage professional who volunteers time and heart for Habitat for Humanity and gets to see firsthand a family who never believed they would ever have their dream home.

- To the sales professional who takes the time to give gifts, not just to clients but to those less fortunate.

- To the United States Marine Corps Reserve for the thousands of toys they distribute each year for the "Toys for Tots" program. The smiles they create are endless as well as the tears of joy they shed.

- To the volunteers that deliver "meals on wheels" for those that cannot leave their homes due to illness and accident. Their hearts are far warmer that the meals!

- To every person who takes even a moment out of his or her day to perform a random act of kindness in the spirit of the heart. The joy given never equals the joy received!

The great English statesman, Sir Winston Churchill said, "We make a living by what we get, we make a life by what we give." Give generously, give gladly, give with laughter and smiles, but most of all, give from the heart and you will never be short on gratitude or joy!

The Greatest Gift

YOU ATTENDED THE last sales rally and some speaker talked about being motivated! In fact, it seems that being motivated is the secret to success. You hear a motivational story and, at least for a few hours, you are ready to finally commit to the dreams you have been putting off! But then it all goes away and once again, you are just trying to make it through the day. How do you sustain the "motivational moments?" How do you get on the path to success and make every day a motivational and productive day? Well, if the answer were easy, everyone would be motivated! The real secret is within everyone's reach, but few people are willing to accept the challenge.

The first step in being truly motivated is to become focused. Most people want to accomplish something, but never truly apply themselves to the task. In other words, they want to reach their dream, but are not 100% committed to the price that must be paid. That is … true focus. Knowing the obstacles and hardships while remaining dedicated to your purpose is critical. As soon as there is a price to be paid, most people give up and say, "Well, it just was not meant to be." Those who are focused fight through the difficult times and eventually triumph.

The second step is unrelenting action. This is taking consistent action toward the goal or dream day after day, week after week, and month after month. It took Jack Nicholson thirteen years to become a successful actor. Robert Frost, the great American poet wrote two decades before he achieved fame. Success is the byproduct of never giving up and never surrendering.

Finally, nothing in this world that is of significance is accomplished without passion. The thing you want must be so important to you and so exciting that you cannot wait to get up in the morning and start a new journey to get that much closer to your dream or goal! Thomas Edison never got tired of looking for new answers and never lost his passion for inventing. When his lab went up in flames one night and everyone was in despair over the loss of equipment and research, he only smiled and said, "Now we can start with new and fresh ideas, a new beginning!"

None of these steps require great intelligence or even special talent. They are traits that every human being possesses, but few are willing to embrace. Start this day and every day with your dreams in mind! Never quit. Never surrender!

Are You Avoiding Difficulties?

IS THERE SOMETHING you should be doing, but you are not? Is there a difficult task you have been avoiding? Does the day go by and you were not able to get that much done? This is not an uncommon situation for any of us. In fact, these situations create stress in our lives when we could be more productive. Avoiding difficult tasks is usually caused by one of the following:

- Lack of knowledge to complete the task: If this is the case for you, look at the project completely and focus on your areas of weakness or consult with someone who has knowledge in this area.

- Not knowing how to get started is common. The correction for this is breaking the project or task down into small workable units. Then only focus on completing one unit at a time.

- Fear of failure. This is an easy one. You will completely fail if you do not get started now! Most of the things we fear regarding failure never materialize! Once again, seek guidance as you begin a difficult task, do your research, and do not be afraid of failure.

- Resentment over being assigned the task. Often we feel others take advantage of us and ask us to do things that should be their responsibility. If you feel this way you might want to analyze the situation and talk to the person involved. It is very possible that he or she is willing to help. In the worst case, you can ask for additional guidance in completing the project.

- Lack of time. We never have time to do all the things in our daily job function. At the same time, we seldom use our time effectively. With major projects it can seem so overwhelming that the easiest thing to do is procrastinate. Try this, put aside 30 minutes each day devoted to your task. You will be amazed at how the time to complete it suddenly appears, especially when you see progress and get excited!

A final pointer in completing difficult tasks is to reward yourself along the way. Set a reward goal for major stages that could be tangible (a nice dinner) or intangible (time off). We are more likely to focus and finish a task when there is an immediate reward for our hard work.

Become a professional who gets things done and you will be recognized by your organization. In fact, these are the people who get promoted and more important who acquire a reputation that is reliable, professional, and dynamic! So what tasks do you need to start today?

Compass or Clock?

HOW DO YOU live your life on a daily basis? Does a compass or a clock guide your life? If you are like most people, you are guided by time. The clock dictates your life based upon deadlines, appointments, things you must do by a certain time, and prearranged places to be such as work, client meetings, or personal agendas. While there is nothing wrong with any of these things, a problem arises when there is no direction in our lives. All of these things become burdens, daily chores that we must do to survive financially, professionally, and personally. As time goes by, certain resentment builds up for having a life dominated by the clock. We find ourselves having too many "have to's" instead of "want to's."

The purpose of a compass is to serve as a guide in pointing the traveler in the right direction. The compass always points in the same direction, true north. This allows the traveler to determine the correct path to follow. If he or she were guided only by a clock instead of a compass, finding the final destination would be by accident, not design. This is also true of the "life traveler." An unguided life is destined to lead any person in an unknown direction. In fact, most of us are letting others guide us down the road of destiny or chance. We lost our compass long ago and are being swept along by our personal and professional commitments. Where does it all lead? If we are lucky, we asked directions enough times that we ended up moderately healthy and successful. But how do we find our "compass" that will guide us to our hopes and dreams? Well, that compass is always with us, hidden deep in our pocket. It is called a "life compass," and it is too often ignored.

Your life compass also has a "true north." This true north happens to be your guiding principles. A guiding principle is what you truly value in your life in order of priority. Try this simple exercise. Write down in order of importance what you truly value. The answers are your true north. If you make all of your life's decisions or directions based upon these values, then it is difficult to get lost in life. As an example, if the highest value on your list was family, that is a guiding principle for direction in your life. The next time your daughter has a soccer game and you put another commitment before it that is not family-related, you have strayed from true north. Sure, things come up and there are exceptions, but if you are sacrificing family on a regular basis, you have lost your life compass and what is truly important is diminished in some way.

Find your compass and you will find more personal fulfillment in your life. Write your values on a small card that can fit into your wallet or purse. Each time you have a choice to make, pull out the card and ask a simple question, "Does this choice follow my guiding principles?" When your life is based upon a compass instead of a clock, you will find that you are seldom lost on the road of life and will certainly enjoy the journey as much as the destination!

Daily Goals

ROBERT SHULER, PASTOR of the Crystal Cathedral in California and one of the great motivators of our time, once asked, "What great dreams would you dare to achieve if you knew you could not fail?" Let's face it, the main reason we do not live our dreams or attempt more in life is our fear of failure. Most men and women live below their achievement level for one reason: the fear that accompanies any attempt of a great task or dream. Ask yourself this: "As a child, what did I want to be when I grew up?" A doctor? An actor? An astronaut? When did you stop dreaming? Although your dreams may have changed since then, if you are like most people, then you still have dreams, even if deeply hidden in your mind. Average people have achieved great dreams and they accomplished the impossible with a simple formula.

1. Acquire a passion! You will never overcome the obstacles to success when they appear, if you do not want to achieve your dream with a burning passion.

2. Write a plan. You cannot achieve your dream until it becomes a goal. Dreams become goals when they are put into writing as part of a plan.

3. Attach daily actions to your plan. For every goal, you must have two to three actions that contribute to the accomplishment of that goal.

4. Start now! Every day you wait, you cheat yourself and drift further away from your dreams and goals.

5.   Take daily action. If you do not attack your goal every day, it slowly eats away at your passion. One day lost is really three: the day you did nothing, the day you could have been one day ahead, and the day you have slipped further behind.

6.   Celebrate small victories! There is no better feeling than when you are moving ahead with a long-term dream or goal and can actually see your progress! Reward yourself in some way as if to say, "I am reaching my greatness!"

7.   Ignore all obstacles! Nothing is a barrier unless you believe it to be. Turn up your intensity when the going gets rough and you cannot fail!

8.   Congratulate yourself on the final victory! (Then start a new goal!)

The great English Playwright, George Bernard Shaw, once said, "People are always blaming their circumstances for what they are. I don't believe in circumstances. The people who get on in this world are they who get up and look for the circumstances they want, and, if they can't find them, make them." Live to laugh, live to learn, leave to win!

Focus on the Invisible

ALL THROUGH LIFE we focus on things that we can see or touch, the "visible" things in life. There are those that focus on the "invisible" and it makes all the difference in the world! Thoughts are invisible, yet the very nature of how we think will form our visible world. Think in negatives and failure, you will receive them ten times over. Dreams are invisible and the minute you stop dreaming those dreams vanish into thin air. In the modern world, our focus on visible things is made evident by television commercials that would have us believe that if we wear certain clothes, makeup, or drink the right product we will be with the "in crowd" or in some way be more content or happy. In other words: the visible. Start thinking in terms of invisible things that can be brought to reality and your world will be filled with all your dreams! Here is a formula to get you started.

- Bring to mind the things you desire with all of your heart. If you think about them often enough, the thoughts begin to become real and the impossible becomes attainable. The great American psychologist William James once said, "If you only care enough for a result, you will most certainly achieve it." The invisible thoughts are the engine of action.

- Once your dreams and goals are daily thoughts, begin to imagine the life you would lead if your dreams and goals are achieved! Ralph Waldo Emerson said, "Be very choosy therefore upon what you set your heart. For if you want it strongly enough, you'll get it." I use the term "Imagineering" to describe this process of living your dream in your mind to help make it reality.

- Put your thoughts on paper and read them daily. Put them in present terms, as if they have already taken place. A goal remains a dream until it is cast upon paper, just like the seed being planted in the soil. Only then can it begin to grow.

- Take small steps every day to get one small step closer to dreams turning into reality. No one started out at the top. They got there one step at a time. Break down your dream or goal into the simplest steps possible and you will find a new enthusiasm for obtaining what might have seemed impossible.

- Think as big as possible! Only large dreams have the power to fuel the soul! People are often afraid of great dreams because the possibility of failure seems so much greater, but it cannot compare to the possibility of success.

Where are you today? Is the visible world of cars, buildings, work, and daily tasks keeping you away from the far more important and rewarding invisible world of thoughts, dreams, and goals that lead to your destiny? Live to Win!

Living Large

HENRY JAMES, THE American novelist said, "Live all you can, it is a mistake not to." It seems most of the regrets of life come at the end when there is little time left to "live large." If your life is filled with "should have's, would have's, might have's, and could have's," maybe it's time to re-evaluate your current position in life. The beauty of life is this … everyone can live large!

Where do you start? How can you start living life to the fullest? It starts with a simple evaluation. Where are you now and where do you want to be? Think of it as a starting line in a race and a finish line. The further away the finish line, the more planning and patience necessary to reach our dreams, to live life to the fullest! Unfortunately, we often wake up in the morning with no plan and little awareness of anything other than "getting through the day." Is it any wonder that most people are only "breaking even" each day?

Try this tonight, write out two things that will help you reach a dream and begin living large. Once you have written these two things down, decide the actions you will have to take tomorrow to get closer to the life you want. An example would be if you wanted to complete your college education. Two "steps" you might take tomorrow would be to go online, fill out an application for admission, and call an academic counselor to discuss options such as night school or weekend programs. "But Ken, I have kids, a job, and I am a single parent?" Well, you are just going to have to work a little harder than the average person, but then, you are not average if you have the courage and are responsible enough to handle all these important duties! The interesting thing is just by taking two action steps it starts a chain reaction. If you will continue two actions every day amazing things can happen!

Accomplishing anything in this world is really all about the patience and persistence to take small actions on a regular basis that lead to "large" results! Getting excited yet? I often tell my coaching clients life is a "to do" list. Unfortunately, most people's "to do" list is filled with "stuff" and not goal-related activities that lead to our greatest dreams. "Stuff" is the things we feel like we have to do. Finishing reports, returning phone calls, solving crisis situations and meetings are all things we must do daily, but most do not help us reach our personal goals. When we add just two things to that list that are focused on reaching dreams, the list suddenly takes on a new life, almost an excitement!

Is the timing not right? I often hear this. "When I finish a certain report or when the kids graduate or when I get that promotion, then I'll focus on my dreams!" Henry James said, "The right time is any time that one is still so lucky as to have." James meant the right time is now when you still have time, when you still have this day, not tomorrow, not next week, next month or next year, right now! Excuses are things we create to avoid failure. Some excuses are legitimate in that they are real and exist, but the successful people in life understand this and take action regardless.

Life rewards us in direct proportion to our contributions. Make no contributions to your dreams and there is no reward. Your life is a bank account and we have the opportunity every day to make deposits and withdrawals. Deposits are every positive action we take and withdrawals are "doing nothing," letting the world pass us by until one day we wake up and wonder, "where did the time go?" Do not let this be you. Live to win!

Overwhelmed?

YOU CANNOT SEEM to keep up anymore! Your house needs cleaning, the kids have activities, bills to pay, friends demanding your time, and, oh yes, what about work? Loan files gone bad, month end reports, irate customers and maybe if you are lucky, time for sales calls! Welcome to the modern world! One thing is for sure, there will never be enough time! No amount of time management seminars or great time management systems will allow you to accomplish everything on your daily agenda. Now the good news. You can accomplish what is most important, if you stay focused on your goals.

I often talk and write about the idea of "goal cards" that you review twice a day. There is a miracle that occurs when you truly focus on the most important tasks on your cards. I had stressed that for every goal you set, there is a set of matching activities. If you truly want to accomplish the things in your life that give you the biggest return, take your goal cards to a new level, simply put a star by the things that will change your life the most and make a point each week to do something toward these life changing activities. Trust me, you will take care of the irate customer, you will solve the loan problems, but little Billy's baseball game will never be played again and the smile on his face will be priceless.

My son played high school football. I never missed one of his football games or important events, even with all the traveling I do as a professional speaker. How did I accomplish this? Great planning and little stars next to every truly important goal! I know it sounds simple, but never forget that the relationships in your life whether business or personal will yield more long term success than all the fires you extinguish every day. (Many of which you created through over-commitment and poor planning!)

I was on a national sales conference several years ago with over 100 loan officers from one of the national retail lenders and the topic was goal setting. We were accepting callers from the nationwide audience. One of the calls was from a loan officer whom I had taken the time to send a thank you card after one of my seminars. He did not have a question. He simply wanted to thank me for the card and taking the time! Point? One of my goals that has a star next to it is to always send a thank you card to people who take the time to speak with me after a seminar. Lesson? Relationship built, impression made, life time opportunities for taking the time to write.

Your business, personal life, and sales will soar if you take time to appreciate and thank clients, family, and friends. Your personal relationships will prosper if you take time to call or write. Your marriage will grow if you are focused on the goal of doing something special for your spouse every week.

There is a song from the 70's (dating myself), titled "Cat's in the Cradle" by Harry Chapin. The song was about a father who never had time for his son. When the son grew up he had no time for his father. Overwhelmed? You will never be more overwhelmed when your greatest goals and dreams slip away, when you have gotten out of touch with your clients, and more importantly those "people," not things that are important in your life. The world's greatest inventor, Thomas Edison, once said, "I have friends in overalls whose friendships I would not swap for the favor of all the kings in the world." Hey! See you on the ball field! And by the way, did you send a card to a friend today? Touch a life and pass it on!

Ripples on the Pond of Life

AS THE YOUNG man sits by the pond, he tosses a small round pebble upon the undisturbed and quiet surface. The clear sheet of glass begins to ripple endlessly. Each small circle grows until it fills the limits of the pond. One after another the ripples continue until, once again, the pond is still and quiet. Curiously, he walks over to a much larger lake and finds a larger stone. Standing over a high bluff, he tosses the stone into the still water below. This time the ripples are larger due to the force of the stone and the concentric circles spread even further with more power until each reaches the shoreline. In a few minutes all is quiet. Was there a lesson to be learned? In fact, there were many.

The stone represents action. There are no ripples until the action is taken. The more powerful the action, the more powerful the result. In life, most people simply look out upon the water. Through fear or through a lack of motivation, the average person never wonders about the possibilities in life and simply watches the lake, hoping, dreaming. Those who do take action often only toss the small stone that is easy to find and the result is mediocre. Those who believe in their dreams search for the largest stone possible. In other words, they make the most valiant effort!

The pond or lake is life itself. It lies before us waiting. It does not care if the stone is tossed or the lake of life remains undisturbed. Once a powerful action is taken, the results echo like the concentric circles upon the lake growing ever larger. Toss only one stone and the ripples eventually subside. Continue to toss stones (unrelenting action), and the results never cease! Life pays us back in kind for the effort we make and it always pays what we ask of it, not a penny more. Try to create small ripples and you get small results. Search for the biggest stone possible, tossed from the highest bluff or ridge, and never stop searching! The greatest achievements in life are born of the greatest efforts. There is no easy way. There is no luck except that which is created by the man or woman of action.

Some people believe that humans are controlled by some destiny, that some are just meant to be famous, rich, or powerful. In truth, the greatest among us create their own destiny by tossing the stones upon the sea of life unrelentingly until the whole world takes notice of all the commotion! Are you the watcher or the doer? Do you blame the world for where you are, just sitting by the lake of life? William Dean Howell said, "An acre of performance is worth a whole world of promise." Let others sit by the lake. It is time for you to begin tossing stones! Live to Win!

Answer the Call

IN THE DAYS when an ice cream sundae cost much less, a 10-year-old boy entered a hotel coffee shop and sat at the table. A waitress put a glass of water in front of him.

"How much is an ice cream sundae?" he said.

"Fifty cents," replied the waitress.

The little boy pulled his hand out of his pocket and studied a number of coins in it. "How much is a dish of plain ice cream?"

Some people were now waiting for a table and the waitress was a bit impatient. "Thirty-five cents," she said brusquely.

The little boy counted the coins. "I'll have the plain ice cream."

The waitress brought the ice cream, put the bill on the table, and walked away. The boy finished the ice cream, paid the cashier, and departed. When the waitress came back, she began wiping down the table and swallowed hard at what she saw. There, placed neatly beside the empty dish, were two nickels and five pennies, her tip.

In today's world we get caught up in what we think matters, missing the opportunities on the path of life to touch another soul, whether a small boy taking ice cream when he wanted a sundae so he would have enough left over to thank the waitress with his last few coins, or a stranger on the street who appears lost or down on his luck.

In John Donne's poem, "For Whom the Bell Tolls," he writes:

Each man's death diminishes me,

For I am involved in mankind.

Therefore, send not to know

For whom the bell tolls,

It tolls for thee.

When the next call from humanity rings out, don't hesitate to act with kindness and caring, after all, we're all in this together. This world can be a stressful place as we work hard to just get through the day. Start taking a few minutes every day to touch a life. After all, when the bell rings, it rings for you!

Necessity

IT WAS THE turn of the century and the telephone was becoming a household item. At the time, no one had telephone numbers, and the Bell Telephone operators actually memorized customer names in order to make telephone connections. All that changed in only a few weeks. In a small town in Massachusetts, the telephone operators became ill with a contagious infection (no one was ever quite sure exactly what it was). Replacements were found, but with one problem. They had not memorized the customers' names and were unable to place telephone calls! One of the callers, a local doctor, had an idea. Why not assign numbers to each of the local residents and have them permanently attached to the switchboard? Because of a contagious illness, the telephone number was born and quickly spread throughout the nation. In the workplace today, many opportunities of necessity exist. Work overload, technology advances, and specialization of job functions create many opportunities for a work team to come up with new ideas to make their team more efficient and profitable. Unfortunately, many employees feel uncomfortable bringing new ideas to the table. This is where leadership comes into play.

Great leadership is the spearhead of new ideas, if leadership follows a few simple practices:

- Constantly encourage people to share new ideas.

- When they share ideas, never discount them. Always be thankful.

- Have brainstorming sessions with no limits! No idea is too crazy! If you get a crazy idea, it may lead you to a more useful one that can solve a problem.

- Reward people, not only for their great ideas, but for their effort as well.

- Ideas that are actually used should be rewarded with a gift or cash!

- Publicly recognize the person who created the idea. Peer recognition is a powerful motivating tool.

- Keep a running total of all ideas presented with the names of the creator. Quantity leads to more useful ideas!

Great leadership encourages and fosters people to go beyond their limits. This can only be accomplished in a safe and trusting work environment where ideas are honored and people are celebrated for their creativity and effort. There is no limit to the heights we can reach!

Risk and Reward

IN ORDER TO make their extraterrestrial more lovable, the producers of the hit movie E.T., met with the M&M division of the Mars Candy Company in New Jersey. They wanted to have ET munch on the famous candy in the movie. M&M, fearing that its candy image would be tarnished if an alien liked it, refused to allow the producers to use the candy.

To find an M&M substitute, the producers met with the H.B. Reese Candy Company and chose a chocolate and peanut butter look alike to M&M's, called Reese's Pieces. You know the rest. The movie was one of the biggest hits of all time and Reese's Pieces became the candy of preference for millions of children!

The problem with M&M was the company was not willing to take risk. In life, the inability to take risk is one of the most limiting factors in reaching your dreams and ultimate success. The beauty of risk is this: if you fail, the knowledge you gain is far beyond that which can be obtained in a book. In fact, the greatest men and women in history failed far more times than they succeeded. People and companies fail to take risk for a variety of reasons. Here are some of the common reasons we do not take risk and with each reason, an answer.

1. We fear failure, embarrassment, financial loss, loss of self-esteem or letting others down. Answer? Always look beyond the risk to the reward. Envision what you are missing by not taking action. Certainly calculate the risk and make sure you have a chance of success, but do not let fear be your negative motivator.

2. Lack of knowledge. We often do not try something because we do not know enough about the task or the procedure to get started. Answer? Break the task or dream down into workable parts and do your research on just the beginning tasks. In other words, take baby steps until you feel more comfortable.

3. Lack of time. This is undoubtedly the most often used excuse in the history of mankind. It has to be the biggest destroyer of dreams that ever existed! There will always be time for what is important in your life. Answer? Put aside specific time to reach your dream, to take that calculated risk. If you do not set a specific time period each day to accomplish your dream, it will never happen! Also, put deadlines on each phase of the task to motivate you to action.

There is little reward in this life without risk. The most rewarding battles in life are those battles that required paying the highest price, making the biggest sacrifices, and taking the most fearful risk. These are the men and women who find the greatest fulfillment.

President Teddy Roosevelt once said, "It is not the critic who counts. Not the man who points out how the strong man stumbled or how the doer of a deed could have done better. The credit goes to the man who is in the arena. Whose face is marred with dust and sweat and blood." You cannot win if you are not in the race of life and the entry fee is risk.

9/11 Remembered

LEE IELPI SPENT months at Ground Zero helping recover the remains of 9/11 victims before they found his son. Jonathan Ielpi, a 29-year-old firefighter with Squad 288 in Queens, was on duty when the first plane hit the World Trade Center. He called his father, who had retired from NYFD Rescue 2 in 1996, to let him know what was going on. "He said, 'That's us, Dad, we're going to the Trade Center,' Ielpi recalls. I said 'OK, Jon; be careful.'" That was the last time they spoke.

Eleven years have passed since the day terrorists flew two planes into the WTC towers in New York, killing nearly 3,000 people, wounding countless others, sparking the war on terror, and whetting the country's appetite for retribution. Although he lost his son that day and witnessed the horror of 9/11 himself, Lee Ielpi is focused on hope, not hatred. "It's so easy to hate," the father of four says. "But I don't understand what we're going to get from hating. I understand justice; I understand the need to get justice. But I don't understand what hating is about."

Continuing to help with the recovery efforts—after they found Jonathan's body in a stairwell in the South Tower, Ielpi spent six more months sifting through the rubble—he became involved with several of the organizations that eventually made up the Coalition of 9/11 Families. Now 67, he is the president of the September 11 Families Association and the co-founder, with Jennifer Adams, of the Tribute WTC Visitors Center, located near Ground Zero.

"On September 10, I was still retired," he says. "My wishes were to go fishing and hunting and hiking and camping and enjoy the outdoors and travel. My family, we were all brought up that way. I was brought up loving the outdoors; my children all love the outdoors. So that was my wish. But 9/11 changed many people, not just me," he says. "My life changed. I had to put most of that on the back burner. Someday maybe I'll get back to fishing and hiking," he adds. "We feel it's more important to continue this mission we're on." Now Lee Ielpi is fighting another battle, cancer from breathing the air at ground zero, but in his mind that is a minor price to pay if he can make a difference.

This week is the 11th anniversary of one of the most tragic days in American history. It is a time to look back but more importantly a time to look forward with hope to a better, stronger country and a nation drawn together to remember those who perished. I recall the words of Abraham Lincoln in the Gettysburg address, "And that government of the people, by the people, and for the people shall not perish from the earth."

Thank you, Lee, for reminding us that it is never about hate and anger, but about justice and hope. That our hearts and minds are focused on building a better world by giving more than we take, by loving more than expected, and by creating positive ripples upon the pond of life that will never stop touching the hearts and lives of others. Pass it on!

Your New Year's Recipe

OKAY. BEFORE YOU get started on the annually frustrating task of committing to New Year's resolutions that are doomed to fail within the first two weeks, why don't you do something different this year? How about a plan? You know, the process where we actually have a step-by-step guide on how we are going to accomplish our goals! This is a simple way to increase your probability of success by taking the time to be serious about what you want to do with our life in a year filled with opportunity. Let's figure this out "recipe style."

Start with a large helping of enthusiasm! It is no secret that the chances of succeeding at any task are in direct proportion to the level of passion we have for the challenge before us. Henry Chester said, "Enthusiasm is the greatest asset in the world. It beats money and power and influence. It is no more or less than faith in action." Interpretation: believe in something so much, we are willing to do something to get it! Enthusiasm and passion attracts the world's treasures to us in a mysterious way that cannot always be explained.

Add in a few ounces of effort! The ancient writer and philosopher Euripides said, "So with slight efforts, how can one obtain great results? It is foolish to even desire it." You cannot lose weight without taking or changing action. You cannot increase your sales without an increase in effort. You cannot get in better physical shape without working out with more effort. There is something wonderful in finishing a difficult task and it is not the finish of the race, it is the amount of effort put forth during the race. Our self-esteem, our satisfaction in life, is built upon the amount of effort that went into a task. Look forward with joy to the opportunity to make great effort and you will gain rewards not granted to most people.

Don't forget your "recipe card." It is also called your written plan. Every study ever done on successful goal setting points to one fact: if your goals are not in writing where you can access them daily, the chances of reaching them are slim. You are preparing a life, a pretty important dish! If you are not looking at your recipe cards daily, you are probably not going to get the result you expected! Why not 3x5 cards that you can put in your purse or in your briefcase? Make a habit of starting your day by reviewing your recipe card and preparing the best life you can every day!

By the way, you might run out of ingredients from time to time. If you get low on enthusiasm, why not call a neighbor and borrow some? To prepare your recipe for success, have backup! Have a person or persons who will support you in your dreams and goals. If you get down or behind, call your backup! Do be careful to choose the best backup possible, the right person or persons who want you to succeed and will cheer you through the toughest times. There is a power in numbers and your backup will enjoy helping you!

Hey! What is it looking like so far? You are excited, your recipe cards are prepared, your assistant chefs (backups) are in place, and you have outlined the daily effort necessary to finish your goal or resolution. What is left? You have to take action—unrelenting, consistent, obstacle hurdling action—day in and day out. Remember, it was not the 1,000th blow of the hammer on the block of granite that split the mighty rock; it was the 999 that came before it. Nothing worthwhile comes easy, but when it comes (and it will!), there is no greater feeling in the world than the achievement of a dream! You are the master chef of your life. Do not let the recipe spoil!

Troubles

DO YOU EVER feel like you just can't go on? Do you ever feel like life's headaches, failures, and obstacles are endlessly parading into your life? The motivational hype will tell you it's not about falling down, but getting up after you fall. For Nick Vujicic that advice has incredible meaning, you see getting up after the fall is a little more difficult for Nick, he has no arms or legs.

Nick Vujicic was born missing both arms at the shoulder and having one small foot with two toes protruding directly from his thigh. Although not mentally impaired, he was not allowed to attend regular schools until the laws were changed. He learned to write using the two toes on his small left foot and also learned to use a computer. He can even answer the telephone and throw a tennis ball.

As you can expect, life was tough growing up and by the age of eight he started contemplating suicide, but one day that all changed. How? By changing his attitude. Nick started to believe he could actually make a difference in the lives of people and they could be inspired by his story. He gave talks to church groups and eventually started a non-profit organization, "Life Without Limbs," to help others who suffer from similar disabilities.

Nick graduated from college at the age of 21 with a double major in Accounting and Financial Planning. He started his own speaking business focused on teenagers, churches, and the corporate sector. His message is one of hope. Nick believes that there is always hope if you focus on a greater purpose for your life. Nick's DVD "No Arms,

No Legs, No Worries" is a reflection of his belief that nothing can stop you if you just believe in your own worth and your own purpose.

It's kind of hard to feel sorry for yourself when you look at all this "twenty-something" young man has accomplished against all odds. In 2008 Bob Cummings interviewed Nick Vujicic on 20/20 where he was able to share his story with the world. His dreams and hopes continue to grow and he hopes to spread his message worldwide.

Was last year a tough year for you? If it was, take great hope that this can be your best year ever, just reflect on Nick's story and compare it to your own. There is no obstacle that life can throw at you that cannot be overcome with a powerful attitude, a good measure of hope, and a lot of good old fashion work. The ancient Roman poet Horace wrote, "Adversity has the effect of eliciting talents which in prosperous circumstances would have lain dormant." If Nick Vujicic had not been born without arms and legs he would have been a very different person, maybe never reaching the goals and dreams that he has created in his life. Take the obstacles, the failures, and turn them into success. Take great motivation from Nick. If he can get up after falling down (yes, he has figured it out, physically) so can you. Never stop believing in the power of attitude, never stop believing in you!

Rainy Days and Mondays

THE HEADLINE FOR this article is taken from the song by the Carpenters. The first stanza sums up the mood of the entire song:

Talkin' to myself and feelin' old
Sometimes I'd like to quit
Nothing ever seems to fit
Hangin' around
Nothing to do but frown
Rainy Days and Mondays always get me down.

It's a classic song but I want to present a different view of "rainy days and Mondays." Call me an optimist or glass half full kind of guy, but I have found that the way we view any given situation is a reflection of the reality we create in our lives. Let's start with rainy days.

Rain represents nourishment and growth. Without rainy days we are in a world of trouble! Rainy days also give us time to reflect on the past as well as time to think about the future. I love standing on my back porch watching a thunderstorm. When the storm is over the air is always a little cleaner (something to do with the lightening changing the ions in the air and the rain grabbing particles of pollution). I don't know about all of that, but I do know I love to take a deep breath after the storm. It makes me appreciate Mother Nature and all of her wisdom! I usually smile before I go back inside. I think next time I will add a bowl of chicken noodle soup and make the moment complete!

Mondays are always unique and every one different and full of hope.

It means I have a whole week to make things right and to accomplish a world of good! I use Mondays to set goals, make my "to do" list, make appointments and write articles like this one. Monday sets the tone for the whole week and I want it to be positive and full of hope and passion. You could go into Monday thinking, "Great, another work week and going through the grind." When you do this you set a negative tone for everything that takes place after Monday. The point is you and you alone determine the attitude you bring into your life. The key word is choice.

Viktor Frankl wrote "Man's Search for Meaning," a landmark book about searching for meaning in even the worst conditions. In Frankl's case it was a Nazi concentration camp in World War II. He was one of the prisoners who had been separated from his family, starved, and nearly worked to death. Frankl noted that the survivors were those souls who held onto hope and a sense of purpose in their lives. Many simply gave up and—usually within day—they passed away. In the death camps everything that made a person human was stripped away. The prisoners were tattooed with a number, starved, diseased, and constantly abused with the threat of death around every corner. Frankly survived and went on to form a new branch of psychiatry. One of his most powerful statements in "Man's Search for Meaning" is this:

"Everything can be taken from a man but one thing: the last of the human freedoms—to choose one's attitude, in any given set of circumstances, to choose one's own way."

In the worst of conditions Viktor Frankl chose life and to use his experience as a guidepost to help and inspire others. None of us face the conditions of the death camps, but when we give away our freedom to choose our attitude, we give up. The winds of fate take over our lives and we become mere victims of our own choice.

I am going to live by a different rainy day song by B.J. Thomas. Here are my favorite lyrics of the song:

But there's one thing I know

The blues they send to meet me won't defeat me
It won't be long till happiness steps up to greet me
Raindrops keep fallin' on my head
But that doesn't mean my eyes will soon be turnin' red
Cryin's not for me
'Cause I'm never gonna stop the rain by complainin'
Because I'm free
Nothin's worryin' me

I hope the next Monday is rainy. I have lots to accomplish! Bring it on!

Unlimited Power

THERE ARE SOME amazing stories. A wife lifts a car off of her husband who is pinned underneath. An author believes so strongly in his book that even after being rejected by more than 100 publishers, he fights on. A broke and unknown actor writes a movie script that is rejected over and over by the studios. When the script is finally accepted on the condition that the author cannot be in the movie, he refuses and continues searching. What do all of these people have in common? They all had a powerful emotional stimulus to succeed at the chosen task and an undying belief in the task at hand.

It is seldom that the most intelligent or most talented achieve great things. No. It is always the person who believes the most, and with that belief, refuses to quit no matter what the odds might be! Ask the author of "Jonathan Livingston Seagull" who was rejected again and again. Ask the writer of "Rocky" who ended up starring in his own Oscar-winning movie and propelling his career to super stardom. These are average people with above-average dreams. These are average people with a strong emotional investment in a dream.

Scientists say we only use about 10% of our true brainpower. Well, for most of us, we probably only use about 10% of our "dream" power too. Dream power is our ability to take a dream and transform it into reality. At the first sign of an obstacle or doubt, we tend to throw in the quitting towel and make one of a number of common excuses. "It was too hard!" "My timing was bad." "I don't have enough time!" "I'll get around to it one day!" Excuses are the pathways that lead to failure. The more we rationalize and make excuses, the more we convince ourselves that we are not meant to achieve our chosen dream.

Here is a simple exercise. Try it and you will be amazed at the outcome! Take a dream that you have and for one week, take some small action every day toward that dream. Make sure it is a true action, not just thinking or writing (unless you want to write a novel!). Spend no less than thirty minutes each day in the action that leads toward your goal. At the end of the week, review what you accomplished. You will be amazed at the results!

The great Helen Keller, blind and deaf since early childhood, once said, "We can do anything we want to do, if we stick to it long enough." When one refuses to quit, failure is not an option, success, in some form, is always guaranteed, and victory is assured! The common person with uncommon valor and passion will rise above the gifted and take his or her place among the souls who know the battle does not always belong to the swiftest, strongest, or most intelligent, but to the one who refuses to quit even after the worst hours of darkness. Seize the day!

The Power of Fear

THE LEGENDARY FOOTBALL coach Bear Bryant of Alabama was always paralyzed with fear before every game. He seldom kept his lunch or dinner down! The great Winston Churchill, one of the greatest leaders and inspiring speakers in history, suffered such stage fright that he would rehearse his speeches hundreds of times. The unique thing about both of these great men is that they faced overwhelming fear on a regular basis and never let it stop them from achieving greatness. Why are some people so paralyzed by fear while others are able to use it as a motivator? It is a matter of how we think and the choices we make!

Fear is the mind's way of alerting us. In fact, psychologists have discovered that fear actually serves to focus the mind very intently. This is the mind's way of preparing to deal with fear. Unfortunately, some people take this focus and use it in a negative way. They focus on everything that could go wrong. This creates a perceived situation, such as a potential sales call, that becomes a convincing argument not to take action.

The mind's next mechanism to enforce this negative thinking is called rationalization. We reason that we are making the right choice and then come up with reasons why we cannot perform the feared task. Result? We do not take action, which eventually leads to more negative consequences. How can you break the negative fear cycle? Try these steps the next time you face overwhelming fear:

1. Take the focus that fear creates and turn it into a positive

opportunity. Focus on the positive consequences that taking action will bring into your life. Athletes use visualization to do this. They visualize performing the task flawlessly and even the applause of the crowd as they triumph. Visualize the next sales call in every detail, including exactly what you will do and the questions you will ask. See a positive outcome!

2.   Break up the feared task into small pieces that you can perform to get you to the ultimate fear. In the sales call example, plan the call and do research on the company or person before you go. Send him or her an article of interest before you arrive, plan how you will get the appointment, and write down all of the questions you intend to ask. By the way, do not forget to set your goal for the call!

3.   Take action as quickly as possible! One true statement about fear is that the longer we feel it and fail to take action, the more real it becomes. Take immediate action!

Fear is like any obstacle in life in that it always appears bigger than it really is, and in most cases, it never comes to reality! Feel the fear and use it for victory!

Motivation by Example

I WAS ON an airplane once and the person next to me asked me what I did. I told him I was a professional speaker and he replied, "You must be one of those motivational speakers that stuff never lasts!"

I replied, "Neither does a bath, but it's a good idea once in a while!"

It is true that motivational speeches are temporary, but they can provide the spark that creates change. In the work place, motivation is a confusing term. The dictionary defines motivation as "movement in a direction." To be motivated is to move to action, to do something. As a leader, one of our tasks is to motivate our team, to create movement in a positive direction. In a real sense, you cannot motivate anyone, but what you can do is create an atmosphere that encourages you team to become motivated. Here is a test to determine if your organization has a motivating atmosphere:

- Are people encouraged to give their feedback, knowing it will always be honored and never criticized? Employees have great ideas, but if their ideas are not listened to and honored, it will not take long before they keep their ideas to themselves.

- Are team members given responsibility and trusted to carry out that responsibility? People want to feel important and one way to create that feeling is to give each team member a unique opportunity to contribute. Maybe one team member each week is responsible for conducting the sales meeting or staying on top of program changes and reporting to the team. People feel important when they are allowed to take responsibility.

- Do you have a reward and recognition system in place that is specific, consistent, and based on what team members want? The simple act of "specific praise" is one of the most powerful things a leader can do to provide a positive atmosphere. Specific praise is far beyond "great job!" The leader is very specific in detailing the action or result the team member accomplished, thanks the team member, and explains the importance of the action.

- Do you create an atmosphere where mistakes are evaluated based on honest effort? Mistakes are necessary for progress and growth. Obviously you cannot tolerate repeated mistakes, especially ones that have legal consequences, but if you do not allow for mistakes, few team members will go the extra mile to take chances that create improvement.

- Does your organization have fun? This is more than the company picnic! Do they look forward to coming to work each day because they truly enjoy what they do? The main reason people change jobs is not money, but their direct supervisor. Take the enjoyment out of what you do and low morale follows! Have an organization that is capable of laughing and enthusiasm for their work will follow.

- Do you walk around on a regular basis, talking to each team member individually and get to know they as people, not just another employee? No one cares what you know until they know that you care! Show them you care!

You as the leader set the tone for your organization. Make sure you are leading by example and that each day you are involved in the lives of team members in such a way that they respect you and will be motivated to perform for you. What's the worst that will happen? You will be happy and successful!

Turning Lemons into Lemonade

ALEXANDRA SCOTT HAD a dream. She started a lemonade stand and dreamed of raising one million dollars. It would seem an impossible dream at best for a little girl, but then again, she was not an ordinary little girl. Someone once said, "Only dream grand dreams…they are the only ones that can truly spark the soul." It is amazing what a little passion, mixed with strong purpose, can do. Average people become superstars, men and women change the world, and yes, little girls reach their dreams!

You see, others felt so strongly about Alexandra's dream that more "lemonade stands" were opened across the country. She raised $2,000.00 her first year and others soon followed totaling over $200,000 in four years. In June 2004, lemonade stands were set up in all 50 states as well as Canada and France. To date, the stands have raised more than $750,000 and Volvo of North America will hold a fundraiser to assure that Alexandra's goal of one million dollars will be reached!

Is there really anything beyond our reach? A little girl believed with her heart and soul and the world responded. Unfortunately, most people quit at the first sign of obstacle or failure, shortchange themselves, and in the end, excuse away their dreams as "not meant to be," or "I'm not good enough." If there is breath, there is hope. If there is a will, there is a way. If there is belief, mountains are moved. One little girl with a big heart decided not to allow the world to steal her dreams and refused to quit!

Alexandra Scott was four years old when she dreamed of her lemonade stand and squeezed the first lemon. Diagnosed with neuroblastoma, an aggressive form of childhood cancer, she knew time was important and certainly did not waste a day. Sunday, August 1, 2004 eight-year-old Alexandra Scott, dreamer, champion of a cause to raise funds to fight childhood cancer, went to sleep and never woke up. She lived a more complete life in eight years than most of us have ever hoped for or have ever dreamed. Maybe it is time you reach for the stars and make lemonade out of lemons?

Words and Actions

IT WAS ONE of those autumn days in the South with a light breeze and the first hint of coolness in the air after that first cold front. I remember thinking what a great night it will be for our first home game in cool, dry weather. Game day was a busy one for me as the high school athletic director and assistant football coach. I was totally preoccupied when the knock came at the door of my office. When I opened the door it was an unexpected sight, one of my former track athletes whom had graduated just three years before.

David had been one of those quiet kids who was not gifted with talent but had an incredible work ethic, the kind of kid you loved coaching even though you knew that a fourth place finish was a good day for David. I shook his hand and noticed right away that it was extremely warm, almost hot, as well as calloused. I gave him a huge and we began to talk. I knew he had moved to Texas and my first question was, "What are you doing here?"

His reply was unexpected. "Coach, I drove all night to come and see you to say thanks for saving my life."

Stunned, I had no idea what he meant until he told me his story. He had been working at an oil refinery in Houston, Texas and one day he was caught in an explosion that left third degree burns over 70% of his body. "Coach, I was in the hospital emergency room going in and out of consciousness and heard the nurses and doctors say, 'He will never make it.' The pain was unbearable but then I remembered what you always told us, that pain was a purifier and could not defeat us unless we let it take over. Coach, I just kept saying over and over, pain is a purifier and was determined that I would win this struggle."

I was in tears.

To the surprise of the doctors and nurses, he survived and in the process he felt his life had been changed forever. I asked him to explain and some very profound words came from this 20-year-old young man.

"I felt a tremendous need to make a difference in the lives of people the way you made a difference in mine."

We shared old stories of both humor and triumph with lots of laughter and smiles added to the mix of emotions. David left about an hour after he had knocked on my door. I walked him outside and watched him drive away, headed back for Texas. I sat on the steps outside Orange Park High School on one of those autumn days that I will never forget. A cool breeze, dry air, clear skies, and deep thought. With tears in my eyes I wondered if I had ever fallen short, if I ever damaged someone through words or actions. I made a resolution on those steps that my words would always be encouraging, that I would treat everyone like a champion and maybe, just maybe, they would become one...just like David. Life is good!

Fear, an Asset

LET'S TAKE A different perspective on fear. Most people believe fear is a negative emotion that is a reaction to the unknown, the dangerous, or that which is threatening to our mental process. If you saw a 600 pound Bengal tiger in front of you that would definitely be a threat! Falling from a building? Dangerous and a threat! Fortunately, these are not the fears we face the most. The fears we face the most have little to do with physical danger and a lot to do with "mental danger." If you fear making a fool of yourself on the dance floor, you probably imagine falling or just looking foolish. There is little risk of physical harm, but a lot of "mental risk."

Here is a different perspective on fear. Think of fear as a hope of success without confidence, education, or practice. What would happen to your fear on the dance floor if you took six weeks of lessons and got constant encouragement? It would diminish greatly! If you feared public speaking, but joined Toastmasters International and got the opportunity to learn and grow in front of supportive peers, what would happen to your fear? You see, without hope there is no mental fear! If we fully believed we could not accomplish a task, we would not attempt it therefore we would not fear it. The slightest ray of hope allows us to look into the future with uncertainty, but with a glimmer of chance. Physical fear is real and built into the human psyche as a protective emotion against harm or death. Mental fear does not consciously recognize the difference and displays all the same symptoms. Want to overcome your mental fears? Here is a simple formula:

• Educate yourself in the thing that you fear. A new job is fearful because we do not possess all the knowledge to function correctly. Put aside time daily to educate yourself about the thing you fear and the fear will diminish!

- Practice! No one learns to ride a bicycle without falling down but eventually the skill is never forgotten. It takes years to train a killer whale to jump out of the water and through a hoop. A great pianist practices for years before he or she is ready for the concert hall. Human beings are wondrous creations. We can learn almost any skill through practice.

- Baby steps! Overcome your fear in small steps. When tight-rope walkers first learn their skill for a circus performance, the wire is placed at ground level. But eventually, through gradually raising the wire, they walk 50 feet above the circus floor!

- Mental rehearsal. If you fear making sales calls, educate yourself in sales, practice your skill and then rehearse (role play) in front of friends or co-workers. Also rehearse in your mind. Positive thoughts lead to positive actions!

- Change your "ray of hope" into confidence that you are fully prepared for the challenge set before you. Confidence is as much a mental state as fear, but more importantly, confidence replaces fear!

So, what makes you fearful? Take this five-step formula and implement it today to overcome your most fearful obstacles. Fear is an emotion that comes solely from within. Attack it with your heart and soul and hope changes into confidence, then confidence transforms into reality!

Focus

WE LIVE IN a world of distractions, many intentional such as television, movies, and concerts. While these are all good things, they are also symbols of the need to occupy time. Young people play video games while in the past they would play outside. More distractions! One of the complaints I get from sales professionals is they do not have the time to make sales calls, even when they are struggling to succeed. I think what the world really lacks is focus. When you read stories of great inventors, or men and women who changed the course of history, each one had an undying focus and passion for one thing: their dream!

It is easy to lose focus in today's world. We have so many obligations and so many choices. One minute we are "focused" on a goal and the next minute we are putting out fires. The day comes to an end and often we wonder, "What did I really accomplish?" Well, there is an answer! Like in all great things, the answer is painfully clear. We must have a burning desire for something in order to maintain long-term focus. The more desire and passion for something, the more focus and sacrifice to obtain it. Unfortunately, we let obstacles and distractions get in the way. No more! Here is your formula for success!

- Have a plan! If you know the steps you have to take to reach success it is easier to know each day what you should be doing. Miguel DeCervantes said, "The man who is prepared has his battle half fought."

- Break your plan down into workable, daily parts that can be executed in small steps. Working toward your goal daily is inspiration in itself. Finishing a small portion of your large task gives you a feeling of accomplishment and a belief you are making progress.

- Start each day with affirmations. Affirmations are positive statements relating to the thing upon which you desire to be focused. "I will contact five new prospects today that will lead me to my goal of closing 24 million dollars in loans this year." This is a simple example of an affirmation of action.

- Get an accountability partner, someone who is willing to contact you on a regular basis and keep you focused on the goals and dreams upon which you should be focused. It is amazing what we will do when we know someone is watching!

- Surround yourself with positive people! One negative person can bring you down, even when they are well meaning. "You should be happy just to have a job!" is a negative statement. Why should you be content in a job that does not inspire you? Positive people are goal-oriented and will pull you forward with them.

- Read and listen to motivational and instructive information. One positive thought leads to another! One thing you read or hear could be your inspiration to reach new levels in your life!

- Think and act if you have already accomplished your goals!

There is nothing earth-shattering about any of these concepts. They are simple, easy to follow ideas that can only magnify your desire for the dreams of a lifetime. No great thing is accomplished without an undying passion for a better tomorrow!

Keep Playing

WISHING TO ENCOURAGE her young son's progress on the piano, a mother took her boy to a Paderewski concert. After they were seated, the mother spotted a friend in the audience and walked down the aisle to greet her. Seizing the opportunity to explore the wonders of the concert hall, the little boy rose and eventually explored his way through a door marked "No Admittance."

When the houselights dimmed and the concert was about to begin, the mother returned to her seat and discovered that the child was missing. Suddenly, the curtains parted and spotlights focused on the impressive Steinway on stage. In horror, the mother saw her little boy at the keyboard, innocently picking out "Twinkle Twinkle Little Star."

At that moment, the great piano master made his entrance, quickly moved to the piano, and whispered into the little boy's ear, "Don't quit. Keep playing." Then leaning over, Paderewski reached down with his left hand and began filling in a bass part. Soon, his right arm reached around to the other side of the child, and he added a running obbligato. Together, the old master and the young novice transformed a frightening situation into a wonderfully creative experience, and the audience was mesmerized.

Whatever the situation in life and history, however outrageous, however desperate, whatever dry spell of the spirit, whatever dark night of the soul, God is whispering deep within us, "Don't quit. Keep playing. You are not alone. Together we will transform the broken patterns into a masterwork of my creative art. Together, we will mesmerize the world with our song of peace."

You might say, "But I am no master! I am like the little boy!" Every dream has a beginning no matter how big or small. The dream starts with a basic idea and very slowly we add our passion and creativity until we reach beyond ourselves. I like to think of life as a construction project. Unfortunately most people have no plan for their project (themselves) and build a life with "construction flaws" that ultimately fail. The greatest artist or inventor had a starting point like the little boy on the piano but few have an ending point like Paderewski.

We all need a big sign around our necks saying "work in progress, please be patient." Maybe the key is to simply keep building and keep playing until we have built our masterpiece, a human life worth meaning and substance, filled with wonder, excitement, joy, and success. Masterpieces come in many forms—from a beautiful garden to a piano concerto—each important, each creating wonder, and each worthy of praise and ultimate joy.

The Three "C's" of Success!

SUCCESS IS A very elusive word and defined by every person in a different way. For some, success is having a happy family and for others, it is related to work or even personal development. At the essence of success, there are three things that allow us to reach our dreams and goals in our chosen area. They are the "three "C's" of success.

1. Compassion: We must have a deep empathy for the world around us. Truly great people are very caring people. Their compassion allows them to contribute to the greater good and have a full understanding of people. This compassion allows them to communicate effectively and create solutions to help others be more successful. When you help others achieve what they desire, you are richly rewarded.

2. Courage: The American writer and philosopher, Ralph Waldo Emerson said, "Troubles and problems have a way of disappearing when courage comes into the picture." When we have the courage to face obstacles and failure and do what we fear, it is then that we grow as a human being. If you review your life experiences, the times you stood with courage are your proudest moments. Courage is a decision, not a talent or gift. Everyone possesses it given the right motivation or circumstance. What parent would not rescue his or her child from danger, regardless of the risk? Bring courage into your dreams and goals and success is close at hand.

3. Commitment: Small goals and dreams do not excite the soul like giant dreams, yet few people pursue their greatest desires because of their fear of failure. Understand the fundamental rule of the universe:

there is no result without an effort. It is never the first strike of the hammer on the stone that breaks it, nor the last. It is the thousand in between. A word that is permanently attached to commitment is persistence, never giving up. How many men and women have fallen short of their dreams when success was only one effort away? They will never know. We live in a society of instant oatmeal, fast food, and movies upon demand. "Instant" does not work with success. Every "overnight" success spent years of preparation to achieve the opportunity to reach the top.

Make compassion, courage, and commitment your constant companions on the road to success. You will never be alone and you will never be uninspired to reach the unreachable. Here is a homework assignment: write these three words on a 3x5" index card and review the words throughout the day. After only a few days, you will find yourself using these words and incorporating them into your daily routine. Even if in a small way, your life will begin to change and so will your attitude. Compassion, courage, and commitment, you will never have more dependable allies!

Hidden Talents

MOST WOULD THINK of him as a typical nine-year-old with no extraordinary talents who is a little on the quiet side. Born in Saginaw, Michigan and transplanted to Detroit, he had some adjustments to make with his new classmates. It helped that he had a very special teacher, Mrs. Beneduci. She recognized something special in the young man from Saginaw. He was bright and not afraid to answer questions. He was a great listener and she discovered he had a very special talent, his sense of hearing! One particular incident brought this fact to light.

It was during a history lesson that the remarkable talent was highlighted. While asking the class various questions a strange noise was heard somewhere in the classroom! No one could quite tell where the squeaking sound came from as everyone listened intently. Very quietly Mrs. Beneduci asked Steve, the quiet, well-mannered nine-year-old to listen for the sound and help locate the source. As the class became very quiet, Steve not only located the source of the sound, but said, "It's a mouse!" The class adopted the small rodent as their mascot and Steve discovered an amazing gift. Was the mouse purposely planted by a very insightful teacher? We will never really know, but she continued to encourage the shy young man to use his gift in the world of music. As with so many people with Steve's gift, the sense of sound is enhanced with another sense is taken away. In the case of Steve Morris it was his lack of sight that gave him such a wonderful ear for music! He would go on to win numerous awards as an adult—Grammy's, over seventeen gold records, four gold albums and four platinum. Yes, this shy young man with the special gift was known to the world as Little Stevie Wonder.

The real story here is not that of a talented musician, producer and songwriter. It is far more than just success, it is the journey. As we travel in life there are very special giving people along the way who—through their selflessness and compassion—lead us like a compass along life's winding path. It is also the story of taking what life gives you and becoming the best you can be. What's holding you back? Within every human being is something special, something unique. As you travel along life's path do it with passion and belief in yourself, after all, there is no one like you!

Oh Say Can You See

HE WAS FROM a well-to-do family. His father was a lawyer, judge, and member of the Continental Army in the Revolutionary War. He lived comfortably on the family plantation and eventually studied law at St. John's College in Annapolis, Maryland.

America was involved in the War of 1812 with Great Britain. The 34-year-old lawyer was assisting British Prisoner Exchange Agent, Colonel John Stuart Skinner. The two men were aboard the British ship HMS Tonnant as the guests of three British officers, negotiating the release of prisoners one of whom was Dr. William Beanes, a resident of Upper Marlboro, Maryland. They successfully negotiated Beans' release but were not allowed to leave the ship since they knew too much about the British strength and position of their troops. The British intent was to attack Baltimore. That evening, September 13, 1814, they dined with the British officers and the young lawyer and his colleagues stood aboard the British ship and watched the bombardment of Fort McHenry.

It was a night of explosions and fireballs as the British relentlessly fired upon the fort. At dawn the young lawyer was wide awake. As the smoke and fog cleared, he saw the American flag flying high over Ft. McHenry and reported it to the prisoners below deck. He was so touched and inspired that he put words on paper and named his work, "Defense of Fort McHenry." It was published in the newspaper "The Patriot" on September 20, 1814 and instantly became a nationally known work.

Eventually the name of the work was changed and adopted as The American National Anthem, first in 1916 by Executive Order from President Woodrow Wilson and then by Congressional resolution in 1931 and signed by President Herbert Hoover. Yes, The National Anthem, "The Star Spangled Banner," was written aboard a British vessel by the attorney at law, Francis Scott Key, and not officially recognized as our nations song until 1931 over 110 years later.

Every American knows the words to the first verse of the song, but perhaps the most powerful verse is the fourth and final stanza. As we think on this special day, Independence Day, let these words be memorized and echo throughout this great land:

Oh, thus be it ever, when freemen shall stand
Between their loved home and the war's desolation!
Blest with victory and peace, may the heav'n-rescued land
Praise the Power that hath made and preserved us a nation!
Then conquer we must, when our cause it is just,
And this be our motto: "In God is our trust":
And the star-spangled banner in triumph shall wave
O'er the land of the free and the home of the brave.

A special blessing and thanks to our devoted military men and women and all they have given for the cause of freedom.

Timing that Changed History

IT WAS A critical turning point in the Revolutionary War. George Washington's Continental Army had been defeated in battle and was held up for the winter in Valley Forge. Disease was rampant, desertion high, and in only a matter of days the enlistment period would be up for most of the men. The army was a rag tag group of militiamen from various colonies in America with little discipline, but a lot of heart. When help was needed the most, it appeared in the most unusual form.

Friedrich Wilhelm August Heinrich Ferdinand von Steuben wandered into Washington's camp. The road to Washington was an interesting one. Baron von Stuben has met the French Minister of War, Claude Louis, Comte de Saint-Germain on travels to Ireland. The count in turn introduced the Baron to Benjamin Franklin who was in France at the time, attempting to build support for the American Revolution. Franklin wrote a letter of recommendation for Baron von Stuben as a "Lieutenant General in the King of Prussia's service." The Baron claimed he could organize Washington's troops into a well-disciplined fighting army before the spring came.

The Baron spoke no English and worked through a French interpreter who then gave the orders in English. The Baron, dressed in full military attire cursed both in French and German with intensity as he pushed the militiamen and successfully organized them into well-trained fighting units. In fact, the Baron's teachings were published in "Regulations for the Order and Discipline of the Troops of the United States," eventually called the "Blue Book" and even included rules and regulations on camp layout and sanitation. The results of his training showed quickly both in The Battle of Barren Hill, May 20, 1778 and then again at the Battle of Monmouth in June 1778. Prior to the Baron's teachings bayonets were used as skewers to cook meat. Steuben's introduction of effective bayonet charges became crucial. In the Battle of Stony Point, American soldiers attacked with unloaded muskets and won the battle solely on Steuben's bayonet training.

Washington got The Continental Congress to approve Baron von Stueben as Inspector General of the Continental Army on May 5, 1778. One man's influence became one of the many deciding factors in the success of the American Revolution. However there was one very interesting fact, Baron von Stueben has never been a Lieutenant General in the Prussia military. Either lost in translation or a matter of pride, von Stuben had never risen above the rank of captain and was discharged from the Prussian Army for unknown reasons. He had to be advanced funds from the French government to make the trip to America. Fortunately George Washington had little use for titles, but recognized results.

After the war Baron von Stuben was granted citizenship and given land and a military pension for his service to the American cause. In many parts of the country they hold a holiday in his name and several monuments still exist honoring his contribution to the American cause.

In history and in life, it is often the most unexpected events that change the course between success and failure. If von Stuben has not appeared 13 days before, most of the Continental Army would have left. It is with certainty the American's would not have won the Revolutionary War.

The Blame Meter

ONE OF THE great inventions of all time would be a "blame meter." Imagine a few wires you hook up to your wrist and every time you blame your misfortunes on something or someone, it registers on the blame meter. In fact, it registers with a warning message that says in a robotic voice, "Warning! You are blaming someone else or circumstances for your problems! You are in danger of self-destructing! Cease your blaming immediately!" Maybe after a while we would stop blaming circumstances and people and start taking responsibility! In today's downsized, and stressful workplace, it is easier than ever to feel unappreciated and overworked. Add family and financial pressures and it is easy to see why some very positive employees would turn to the "blame game."

What are the dangers of "blaming?" If we do it enough, we actually start to believe we are right! At that point, reality becomes distorted and any hope of success, much less happiness, becomes a distant dream. Sure, you will still get through life, but you will lose any chance of reaching the "giant dreams." The ones that inspire the soul. "My boss is the problem, he/she gives me very little support." "If my wife/husband would just stop nagging me!" "It's not my fault my sales are down, the company doesn't do any advertising!" The list goes on endlessly for the people who would rather "excuse their lives away."

Actually, we do have a "blame meter." It is called reality. Somewhere deep in the recesses of our mind, we know that ultimately we are responsible for our own success or failure in any given circumstance. If we are determined to reach our goals and dreams, taking responsibility for the reality of our choices (to blame or not to blame), is a key step in the truly successful life.

The great writer, George Bernard Shaw wrote, "People are always blaming their circumstances for what they are. I don't believe in circumstances. The people who get on in this world are the people who get up and look for the circumstances they want, and, if they can't find them, make them." What a powerful statement! Put simply, if you spend time shaping your destiny instead of letting the world shape it for you, the world's riches come to you in abundance.

Turn your "blame meter" on full power, determine to shape your reality as you would like it to be and there is no limit to what you can accomplish! When we stop blaming circumstances and people for our limitations, we elevate ourselves above the level of ordinary into the realm or champions. Once you stop blaming, action takes over your daily life. Action leads to a positive self-image, self-image leads to positive attitude, a positive attitude leads to unlimited energy and purpose, transforming our world above the ordinary life that most people resign themselves to live. Live to win!

It's Only a Game...or is it?

THERE WAS AN unusual high school football game played in Grapevine, Texas. The game was between Grapevine Faith Academy and the Gainesville State School. Faith is a Christian school and Gainesville State School is located within a maximum-security correction facility.

Gainesville State School has 14 players. They play every game on the road. Their record was 0-8. They've only scored twice. Their 14 players are teenagers who have been convicted of crimes ranging from drugs to assault to robbery. Most had families who had disowned them. They wore outdated, used shoulder pads and helmets. Faith Academy was 7-2. They had 70 players, 11 coaches, and the latest equipment.

Chris Hogan, the head coach at Faith Academy, knew the Gainesville team would have no fans and it would be no contest, so he thought, "What if half of our fans and half of our cheerleaders, for one night only, cheered for the other team?" He sent out an email to the faithful, asking them to do just that. "Here's the message I want you to send," Hogan wrote. "You're just as valuable as any other person on the planet."

Some folks were confused and thought he was nuts. One player said, "Coach, why are we doing this?" Hogan said, "Imagine you don't have a home life, no one to love you, no one pulling for you. Imagine that everyone pretty much had given up on you. Now, imagine what it would feel like and mean to you for hundreds of people to suddenly believe in you."

The idea took root. On the night of the game, imagine the surprise of those 14 players when they took the field and there was a banner the cheerleaders had made for them to crash through. The visitors' stands were full. The cheerleaders were leading cheers for them. The fans were calling them by their names. Isaiah, the quarterback/middle linebacker said, "I never in my life thought I would hear parents cheering to tackle and hit their kid. Most of the time, when we come out, people are afraid of us. You can see it in their eyes, but these people are yelling for us. They knew our names."

Faith won the game, and after the game the teams gathered at the 50-yard line to pray. That's when Isaiah, the teenage convict-quarterback, surprised everybody and asked if he could pray. He prayed, "Lord, I don't know what just happened so I don't know how or who to say thank you to, but I never knew there were so many people in the world who cared about us." On the way back to the bus, under guard, each one of the players was handed a burger, fries, a coke, candy, a Bible, and an encouraging letter from the players from Faith Academy.

It is the sincere acts of unselfish kindness you perform that will ultimately define you. Go the extra mile to touch lives and you will never be short on true riches. Stand up and make a difference!

Good to Great

WHETHER YOU ARE a business owner, parent, student, athlete, or you work for someone, there is always a lingering question that at some time in your life you will ask yourself, "How do they do it? How do some people reach greatness while most of mankind just gets by?" Our train of thought will then jump to what could have been or possibly a dream you gave up long ago. In the end you convince yourself that you are just not one of those chosen ones. What is it that creates monumental success whether a billionaire business tycoon, a famous actor, or even a novelist? Surprisingly the same key factors.

It starts with an unbridled passion for "the one thing." The ultra successful businessperson is usually not motivated by money, but rather an idea or concept they believe will change the world. Bill Gates' passion for technology was so great that he dropped out of school to pursue his dreams. Walt Disney went bankrupt several times, but refused to give up on his dream of the animated cartoon. The average person believes he or she is passionate, but in reality the average person will fold at the first sign of difficulty or make excuses about why their dream is not possible to achieve. Mia Hamm, Olympic soccer star and women's FIFA Player of the Year in 2001 and 2001, was born with a club foot and had to wear corrective shoes as a small child. This never stopped her from reaching her dream. She said, "If you don't love what you do, you won't do it with much conviction or passion." Don't read any further if you don't have a passionate dream to pursue, you will never pay the price.

The second factor is immunity to failure. Failing at anything hurts, especially when it involves something you value. Most people can't take that kind of psychological pain and would rather make excuses than face the pain head on. Winston Churchill said, "Success is stumbling from failure to failure with no loss of enthusiasm." Imprint these words in your brain forever. The next time you are ready to give up, remember there is no success without massive failure. Napoleon Hill, the author of "Think and Grow Rich," said, "Every adversity, every failure, every heartache carries with it the seed of an equal or greater benefit. You have to embrace failure as a necessary component of success and it will funnel you to an ultimate vision that will allow you to reach your dreams."

The final factor is perseverance. The dictionary definition of perseverance is "continued effort to do or achieve something despite difficulties, failure, or opposition: the action or condition or an instance of persevering: steadfastness.

Sir Thomas Buxton, a British politician from the 1800s said, "With ordinary talents and extraordinary perseverance, all things are attainable." Refusing to give up on a viable idea or talent will ultimately lead to great triumph." The world is filled with unlikely "superstars."

Passion, immunity to failure, and perseverance are a winning combination that will change your life forever. The ancient Chinese philosopher Confucius wrote, "Our greatest glory is not in never falling, but in rising every time we fall." Set your goals high, believe beyond your dreams, and live to win!

Run to Win!

ON MAY 6, 1954, he came to the Iffley Road track in Oxford for the annual match between the Amateur Athletic Association and Oxford University. Windy and raining, conditions were far from ideal. A considerable crosswind blew across the track as the mile race was set to begin. There was no particular goal that day, except to win the race, the one mile run. What happened next was one of the most famous events in sports history. The athlete who stepped on the cinder track that day—intending to simply run his best—became the first man to break the four-minute mile barrier.

Many "experts" of the time said that it was physically impossible for a human being to run a mile in less than four minutes, but then great athletes seldom listen to experts. Young Roger Bannister had been disappointed by not winning the 1952 Olympic Games in the 1500 meters and in the back of his mind was looking to redeem himself. He told reporters after the race that he had been thinking about the four-minute mile barrier but did not think this race had the ideal conditions to accomplish the impossible. When Bannister crossed the finish line in 3:59.4 seconds he did more than achieve the impossible, he shattered a widely held belief.

Perhaps the biggest lesson in Bannister's performance is that most limitations or beliefs are self-imposed within the mind and spirit of each human being. By Bannister leading the way, he changed the mindset of those around him. In just over one year after his performance, four other men broke the four-minute mile record. The greatest limitation was not the physical ability of these athletes, but rather a mental barrier that, once broken, allowed others to believe. Here is a simple formula for accomplishing the impossible: P+P+B=S or Passion + Persistence+ Belief = Success!

Few great feats are accomplished without a burning desire to accomplish the chosen task. Passion is an undying energy that propels us to new heights, gives us the strength to rise after falling, and makes us blind to the advice of critics. However, passion dies quickly without a "roll up your sleeves" attitude that says "never quit, never surrender."

President Herbert Hoover had this to say about never quitting:

"Nothing in the world can take the place of persistence. Talent will not; nothing in the world is more common than unsuccessful men with talent. Genius will not; unrewarded genius is a proverb. Education will not; the world is full of educated derelicts. Persistence and determination alone are omnipotent."

The book "Think and Grow Rich," by Napolean Hill says it best, "Whatever the mind of man can conceive and believe can be achieved." Do you have that one goal that has been eluding you? That one dream that returns to your mind late at night? Today is the day to break your four-minute mile, whether it is writing a novel or losing weight, acquire a passion for achieving your goal, be persistent in the application of your effort, and there is little doubt that you will succeed, but it starts today...not tomorrow, not next week. Today!

Fido the Dog

EVER WONDER WHERE the name "Fido" came from regarding dogs? Fido is a Latin word meaning "I trust." When it comes to dogs, most of us would agree that you can trust your dog! Throughout history, starting with the Romans, the name "Fido" became synonymous with our canine friends. I guess another word for Fido could also be interpreted as faithful and that brings us to one dog story that stands out in history. In fact, the dog's actual name was Fido.

It was a winter evening in 1941, not far from the city of Florence, Italy in a small town called Borgo San Lorenzo. A factory worker named Carlo Soriani returned home from work when he heard yelping. He discovered an injured little puppy, took him home, and nursed him back to health. They became the best of friends and the dog began to follow Carlo everywhere he went. That's when he decided to name the dog "Fido," based on his undying faithfulness. One of the places Fido would follow Carlo was to the bus stop where every workday Carlo would catch the morning bus to his job. Fido would hang around until evening when his master would return to the bus stop, always overjoyed to see Carlo.

The ritual of Carlo and Fido walking together to that same bus stop went on for two years until December 30, 1943. The allies were bombing the factories in Italy and Carlo Soriani was tragically killed on that faithful day. Fido met the bus that afternoon, but the joy of meeting his master would never come again. Eventually he returned home to Carlo's wife. The next day Fido returned to the bus stop at the usual time only to be disappointed again. Fido met Carlo Soriano's evening bus the next day, the next week, the next month, the next year and the next decade, every single day for fourteen years, almost 5,000 times.

The story of Fido spread throughout Italy, Europe, and the world. In 1957 a ceramic statue was erected in the town to honor the faithfulness of Fido, but vandals destroyed the statue. The town then commissioned the Italian artist Salvatore Cipolia to create a bronze statue that still stands today. Fido passed away in June of 1958, alone, on a rural road outside of town. He was buried with honors just outside the cemetery of his master. His passing was a major news story.

In today's fast-paced world it becomes so easy to grow immune to the "defining moments" in life when we can pause and take in the wonders of this world. Whether the undying loyalty of a dog, to the amazement and wonder of a starry night. The story of Fido is far more than an animal returning to a bus stop for 14 years, it is a longing in our hearts to believe in the goodness and faithfulness that still exists if we only take the time to be touched by what is truly important in the universe. Thank you Fido and Carlo for making us remember what is important in life.

Ice Cream Anyone?

IT ALL STARTED in a seventh grade gym class in 1963. The two young boys were not what you would call over achievers or models of athletic ability. They were both chubby and socially awkward. One of the boys, looking back, describes themselves this way, "We were nerds, smart kids who had no social skills. We were fat." Both had moved and were new to Merrick Avenue Junior High School and suffered the typical humiliation of junior high gym class. They ended up in the same phys. ed. Class and found themselves running the mile, both far behind the leaders and dead last. The coach yelled out, "Gentlemen, if you don't run the mile under seven minutes you will have to run it again." The reply from Ben, one of the boys was, "Gee coach, if I don't do it under seven minutes the first time, I'm certainly not going to do it in under seven minutes the second time." From that point on their friendship was sealed!

The two became close friends through high school. One of the young men had a high draft lottery number and decided to drop out of college, the other graduated from Oberlin College in Ohio. After college they both worked odd jobs from custodian to cab driver. In the late 1970s, after being fed up with the lack of direction in their lives, they decided to move to Vermont and start their own business. They wanted to do something food-related since they were both self-professed "eaters." Their first idea was a bagel shop, until they found that the startup cost for equipment was over $40,000. They settled on taking a correspondent course in ice cream-making from Penn State. The rest is history!

Ben and Jerry moved into an abandoned gas station near the University of Vermont and started mixing up gallons of ice cream in an old rock salt ice cream maker using only natural ingredients except for the Heath Bar Crunch. As Jerry confessed, we couldn't help ourselves, we love the stuff! Their ice cream was different, much denser, and about two pounds heavier per gallon. They were an overnight hit with people standing in long lines to buy their incredible ice cream. To make the wait more pleasant, they hired a pianist to play tunes and projected movies onto the side of the gas station.

They began delivering hand scooped pints of ice cream in an old VW bus (what else!). By 1980 they employed over twenty people and started wholesale distribution to stores. A "Time" magazine cover story spread the word even further by saying, "What you must understand at the onset is that Ben & Jerry make the best ice cream in the world." They opened stores and wholesale distribution worldwide.

Their corporate policies were refreshing. One rule was the top corporate executive could not make more than seven times the salary of the lowest paid employee. Jerry is the companies self-proclaimed "Minister of Joy," in charge of employee parties and games. Some companies say that employees are their greatest asset but at Ben & Jerry's it is lived every day. 7.5% of their pre-tax profit goes to charity and "do-good groups." One of their stores in Harlem was connected to a homeless shelter, giving jobs to the occupants and 75% of the profits to the homeless shelter. Many of their flavors represent a chance to give to worthy causes like the "Rain Forest Crunch" of which 40% of the profits are donated to worthy causes.

Ben & Jerry will tell you that the business does not exist to make a profit, it exists to create worthwhile change, to make the world more equitable, just and fair. On their way to making a difference they made a lot of profit. The moral is a simple one, do the right thing, make a quality product, treat people and the world with honor and respect. Success will always follow.

Homeless to Harvard

THE DAY STARTED early for Dawn Loggins. Her custodial job not only required her to work during the evening hours but also early mornings since she worked at Burns High School in Lawndale, North Carolina and had to work around the school schedule. You see Dawn was a student at the school where she worked. Not only was she a student, but an exceptional one, taking advanced placement and honors classes and maintaining a straight "A" average. All this despite a home life that was not exactly ideal.

Dawn's home life consisted of parents who were drug addicted, living in a dilapidated trailer with no electricity or running water. Dawn and her brother Shane would walk to a public park just to fill up water jugs. It was not uncommon to go weeks without a bath. None of this affected her school life. She studied constantly even when she was performing her janitorial duties. She was meticulous on those duties as well wanting to make sure she gave 100% in cleaning the classrooms, hallways, and bathrooms.

Burns High was Dawn and Shane's forth high school, always moving from town to town. In most cases they were evicted. When they arrived at Burns, guidance counselor Robyn Putnam saw the potential in Dawn and enrolled both children in online classes to catch up with the other students.

The summer before her senior year, Dawn was invited to attend a prestigious six-week residential summer program, the Governor's School of North Carolina, at Meredith College in Raleigh, 200 miles east of

Lawndale, to study natural science. It was a field Dawn had never studied before. The program is reserved for the state's top students.

Putnam ferried Dawn to Raleigh to attend the elite program and took her shopping, making sure she had the clothes she needed. Other faculty members contributed funds, too. While at the program she kept trying to get in touch with her parents, but the message said the phone had been disconnected. When she returned to Lawndale, she learned the truth. Her grandmother had been placed in a homeless shelter, her brother Shane had run away, and her parents abandoned the family and moved to Tennessee without a note or word. Dawn was homeless.

The community of Lawndale stepped up. The guidance counselor Robyn Putnam knew Dawn was a step away from being placed into social services custody only to be moved again. Dawn desperately wanted to graduate from Burns High School. She was involved in activities, had a boyfriend, and was a model student. Custodian and school bus driver Sheryl Kolton was called upon to take Dawn into their home and she did.

Settled in with a roof over her head, it was time to do the unthinkable. Apply for colleges. She applied to four in-state schools; University of North Carolina, North Carolina State, Davidson and Warren Wilson College. She did send one out of state school application and with it, a prayer. Soon the acceptance packets starting coming, thick packets with her acceptance letters and mountains of brochures, but nothing from her out of state application. A few weeks later, the letter came from her "other choice." It was a small thin letter, the kind that has a simple rejection letter. She opened it and began to read:

"Dear Ms. Loggins, I'm delighted to report that the admissions committee has asked me to inform you that you will be admitted to the Harvard College class of 2016. ... We send such an early positive indication only to outstanding applicants..."

She was stunned! She had been admitted to one of the most prestigious colleges in the nation. Not only admitted, she was given a full scholarship covering room, board, tuition and books as well as the guarantee of an on campus job.

The world is filled with people, young and old, who become victims of their circumstances. They blame their failure on their background and conditions, yet here is a young lady who by all accounts should be a failure. She places blame with no one including her parents and takes full responsibility for her actions. By the way, she finished her first year at Harvard with flying colors and loves college life. Now it's your turn. What was that dream you never accomplished or that goal unfinished? Live to win!

Saved!

IT WAS THE summer of 1913 and Clarence A. Crane, a candy manufacturer in Cleveland, Ohio, was struggling. His line of chocolates did not travel well in the hot summer months and his sales dropped to almost nothing. To stay in business he decided to develop a line of hard mints. Unfortunately his factory was only set up for chocolates. He decided to sub-contract the job of making the mints to a pill manufacturer. Unfortunately, the pill maker's machine was malfunctioning and kept punching a hole in the middle of the mints. Despite their best efforts the problem could not be fixed. Mr. Crane took one look at the mints and was struck by the fact they looked like small lifesavers. He decided to leave the hole and at the same time had found a name for his new candy! He named it Crane's Peppermint Life Savers and marketed them as a "cure for bad breath."

An ad salesman, Edward John Noble who sold ad space on New York street cars happened to see and taste the new Life Saver candy. He was so impressed that he took a train to Cleveland to convince Clarence Crane to buy ad space for his candy. He told Crane, "You will make a fortune." Crane was not interested, after all, he considered the mints as a sideline to his real product, chocolates. To get rid of Noble, Crane suggested sarcastically that he buy the Life Saver brand if he was that sure. In fact, Crane even offered to throw in the defective pill manufacturing machine. When Noble said, "How much?" Crane was caught off guard and blurted out "$5,000!" Noble thought the price was a steal, but he did not have that kind of money. He went back to New York, raised $3,800, returned to Cleveland, and made an offer at $1900 giving himself a $900 cushion. Crane agreed to the terms.

Noble immediately started running into problems. The candy he had tasted was fresh, but after only a few weeks, the candy absorbed the taste of the cardboard with which it was wrapped. To solve the problem Noble used tinfoil and it worked. However the candy stores demanded that he take back the old candy in exchange for the new ones, which he did. Still sales were extremely slow and he was running low on funds. Unless he did something drastic his candy business would be on "life support." He started convincing owners of drug stores, saloons, barber shops and even restaurants to stock his candy, but with a twist. He created displays that he wanted next to the cash registers and suggested that the cashiers sell the 5-cent candy by giving customers their change in nickels. It worked and the candy became a sensation. Edward John Noble had created the first "check out display."

The company expanded its line far beyond the "Pep-o-mint" and Life Savers and became the biggest selling candy in the world. Since 1913, the company has sold over 44 billion packs. Edward John Noble's vision, creativity and passion, combined to create monumental success. Clarence Crane lacked these qualities but Nobles, the man on a mission, succeeded. What about you? Now many great ideas never saw the light of day because you did not pursue them with vision, creativity, and passion?

Ambition/Passion is the pathway to success but persistence is the vehicle that gets you to your final destination. Enjoy the ride!

An Unlikely Hero

HE WAS BORN on December 13, 1887 in a two-room log cabin near Pall Mall, Tennessee, the third of eleven children. The sons attended school for only nine months. The father wanted them to help work the family farm and hunt for small game to feed the family. Totally impoverished, making ends meet was a day-to-day, month-to-month struggle. The father died in 1911 leaving 14-year-old Alvin to become the man of the house since the two older sons had married and moved away. He worked odd jobs as a railroad worker and logger to feed the remaining eight siblings and his mother. Although a hard worker, he was also a violent alcoholic prone to fighting in saloons and garnered multiple arrests for disorderly conduct.

Despite his drinking and fighting, he attended church on a regular basis. A revival meeting at the end of 1914 led to a total transformation of young Alvin on January 1, 1915 and his fighting and drinking days ended forever. His church was centered on the doctrine of nonviolence. He became a man of peace. World War I would test his faith. He was required to register for the draft on June 5, 1917 at the age of 29. He registered as a "conscientious objector" and not willing to fight based on his religious beliefs. His status was denied and he was sent to Camp Gordon in Georgia. His pastor and mother wrote letters explaining his beliefs and his status as the sole supporter of his family, but something changed.

Deeply troubled by his vow of non-violence and defending his country, he counseled with his company commander, Captain Edward Danforth and his battalion commander, Major Gonzalo Buxton, a devote and religious man. After numerous discussions they granted his a ten-day pass to go home and make up his mind, fully supporting the young man. He returned to camp convinced of his duty to fight for his country. His skill at hunting and expert marksmanship would serve him well.

During an attack to capture German positions, a group of men led by Sergeant Bernard Early; four non-commissioned officers (Alvin now a corporal was among them) and thirteen privates, were ordered to infiltrate behind German lines to take out machine gun nests that had the battalion trapped. The group overran a German unit, capturing a large group of German soldiers. While guarding the prisoners, they were suddenly sprayed with machine gun fire killing six Americans and wounding three others. The loss put the young corporal in charge.

During the assault, six German soldiers charged Alvin and between his rifle and Colt 45 automatic pistol he shot all six before they could reach him. The German officer in charge emptied his pistol trying to kill the American corporal. Seeing his mounting losses at the hands of one man, he surrendered. In all, Corporal Alvin York and his small group captured 132 prisoners and silenced all the German machine guns. York himself had killed 20 German soldiers with his sharp shooting ability.

Alvin York was promoted to sergeant and the awards soon followed. He was awarded the "Distinguished Service Cross." Several other nations granted him their top awards for bravery and General John J. Pershing, head of the American forces, personally awarded him the "Congressional Medal of Honor." He became known as the greatest American hero of World War I.

His heroics went unnoticed in the United States press until a story in the "Saturday Evening Post" made him a national hero. York refused offers to profit from his national and world fame and only lent his name to charitable causes. The only gift he did accept was a 400-acre farm. In the 1920s, York formed the Alvin C. York Foundation to increase educational opportunities in his home state of Tennessee. After many ventures, both successful and unsuccessful, he attempted to reenlist in the military when World War II was declared, but at the age of fifty-four years old he was denied enlistment as a combat soldier and was commissioned a major in the Army Signal Corp. He also worked tirelessly to raise money for the war effort and to support the Red Cross.

York died in a Veterans Hospital in Nashville, Tennessee on September 2, 1964. His wife Gracie sold most of the farm to the State of Tennessee and is now open as the Sgt. Alvin C. York State Historic Park.

On this special day we honor all of our military and endless unsung heroes that have helped to protect and defend this great nation. We will forever remember the backwoods farmer, with no formal education who became not only a brave and unselfish soldier, but a defender of youth and a contributor to the American way.

The Last Basket

IT IS A small college tucked away in the suburbs of Cincinnati, founded in 1920 by the Sisters of Charity. The inaugural class was only 20 students. Fast-forward to today and the school has grown to one of the top academic universities in the nation. It is called "The Mount," and something has happened at this Division III, non-athletic scholarship institution that cannot be explained in simple words. There is a spirit of togetherness, an outpouring of love and caring, but most of all an appreciation for life that has spread beyond the campus, into the greater Cincinnati community, Ohio and the nation. What, or who, has created this magical transformation? It can be explained in two words. Lauren Hill.

This freshman basketball player at Mount Saint Joseph's University has caused quite an uproar that has impacted millions of people across the nation, not because of what she did, but because of what she didn't do. You see Lauren refused to quit when she had every right to quit. This young lady suffers from a rare brain tumor that spreads its cancerous cells throughout the brain, making it inoperable. Don't expect any self-pity from this brave young lady, but do expect to be inspired. Even the NCAA thought so much of her story that they allowed the opening 2014 women's basketball game to be moved up by two weeks to allow Lauren to participate, since the disease is spreading rapidly.

The game versus Hiram College tipped off and the opening basket was a layup by Lauren! The sold out arena seating 10,000 at Xavier University was in an uproar with a standing ovation. What was even more miraculous was the right-hander made the shoot with her left hand since the cancer had made it difficult to shoot with her dominant hand. In attendance was Pat Summitt, former head women's basketball coach at Tennessee and a group of WNBA players. Lauren also made the final basket of the game, which "The Mount" won 66-55. That was not the end of the night, Lauren was awarded the U.S. Basketball Writers Association's "Pat Summitt Most Courageous" award, normally give at the Women's Final Four. Her inspiring words regarding her disease were, "We're gonna fight this."

The national outpouring has been overwhelming. Not one to give up, Lauren Hill started an online layup challenge that involves spinning around five times and shooting a basketball with the non-dominant hand. Fundraising for "The Cure Starts Now Foundation" has raised over $40,000.

One touching moment before the game was from Cynthia Towne, age 11, who is undergoing chemotherapy for a different form of cancer that she has had since the age of 4. With a huge smile she gave Lauren a handmade headband with the words "Believe" and a yellow ribbon in the middle.

Lauren fights on as the disease continues to advance. Lauren announced this Wednesday that she is giving up the game she loves to participate in a different game...the game of life and death. She has been made an honorary coach of her team. Her college career ended with only four games and 10 points, but it will be four games remembered for a life time. She is now in Hospice care, not waiting to die, but determined until the very end to make a difference through her foundation to help others and her goal to raise one million dollars.

We will all face death at some time but the hope is we will leave a legacy of the good we did for others. In a short time, Lauren Hill has left a legacy that will last for generations. Wipe away your tears, she wouldn't want you to cry, but she would want you to make a difference...pass it on.

Having Vision

THE USA TODAY, in 2005, ran a series of articles ranking the most difficult sports in the world. Hitting a baseball was ranked number one, driving a racecar was number two, and number three was pole vaulting. Think about it, you are running with a fiberglass pole in hand, putting it into a tiny box in the ground, bending the pole and then hoping you land in a foam pit! It is that one event that requires endless hours of practice, incredible courage, and perfect technique. From 1982 to 1997, thirteen male athletes died from high school pole vault injuries and there have been numerous permanent, catastrophic injuries. Now add one more element to the dangerous and difficult event, being legally blind.

That's where Texas High School pole vaulter Charlotte Brown of Emory Rains High School comes into the picture. Brown has 20/400 vision in one eye and only a pinhole field of vision in her left eye, yet she has managed to clear 11'6" which would be a great height for a senior much less a tenth grader. In order to run straight and time her vault, she uses an artificial strip alongside the vault runway with contrasting colors and counts her steps to get the pole timed to hit the vaulting box.

Charlotte first starting losing her eyesight as a sixth grader. Doctors could not explain why it happened, but it never stopped Charlotte, a straight "A" student. With her sophomore season over, she will travel to Morristown, New Jersey to receive her first seeing eye dog.

She made the state final meet for Class 3A in Texas for the second straight year and jumped 11'0," which got her fourth place. Still, she received a standing ovation from the crowd. "It's crazy," she said. "I never thought that just doing something so fun, the pole vault, would be something that would inspire people."

Her courage earned her the National High School Spirit of Sport Award last year as a sophomore. This is an award given to only one athlete each year by the National Federation of State High School Associations. The criteria is an athlete who:

- has demonstrated exemplary sportsmanship and/or citizenship in playing the game as it should be played;

- has exceeded normal expectations in assisting others within the school or community; or

- has overcome adversity or a challenging circumstance.

Charlotte wins on all three categories! Life is never about obstacles and handicaps; it is about how we overcome them. The greatest limitation most of us will ever face is the limitations of our own mind. Henry Ford said it best, "Whether you think you can or you think you can't, you are right." The unlimited power that resides within us can only be unleashed through throwing aside the internal doubts, ignoring the critics in life, and driving forward with passion and belief that your dreams are reality if you reach for the stars. Charlotte, thanks!

Little Margy

SHE WAS BORN, in Butte, Montana in 1916 to a family of entertainers. The mother and father performed at a local vaudeville theater in Butte. By the age of three, little Margy Reed was a hit and a natural entertainer. She was so popular that Margy starred with her little brother Bud in the Margy and Bud Show. Show business got in the way of her education and she never got beyond the 5th grade.

A gifted singer as well as actor, by the 1930s she was the lead vocal with the Paul Ash and Boris Morros orchestras. Margy broke into motion pictures in 1934 and by 1936 was cast in comic roles by Paramount Pictures. Over the years she starred with such Hollywood legends at Bing Crosby, Abbott and Costello, W.C. Fields, Charlie Chaplin and many others.

When World War II broke out she felt compelled to join the USO and entertain the troops overseas. This dedication extended to the Korean War and the Vietnam War. She, more than any other entertainer, was truly involved with the men and women on the battlefield and in October of 1966 one incident became a defining moment for Margy. As a helicopter pilot recalled the incident:

"Shortly after her arrival the men were called into combat. Rather than leaving, she kept her group of entertainers at the base, refusing to leave until the men returned and she could give them a show. A helicopter returned to the base at Soc Trang (Vietnam) with several wounded soldiers and officers on board. She sprang into action and volunteered to assist the doctor with the wounded servicemen.

When everyone was back and available, she put on her show. The men loved and admired her for this."

During the war she was made an honorary Green Beret because she visited the United States Army Special Forces without fanfare or publicity. When things got bad and the wounded were brought in she always rolled up her sleeves and became an assistant to the doctors. She became affectionately known by the Green Berets as "Colonel Maggie."

After the wars she went on to star in television and even had her own variety show on television. She appeared on dozens of television shows and movies.

On November 2, 1993 she was awarded the Presidential Medal of Freedom by President Bill Clinton for her service to American troops, the highest honor that can be bestowed upon a civilian. Her unselfishness, devotion to the common soldier, assistance with the wounded, and her passion to help were never forgotten by thousands of former military.

She died on October 19, 1994 and special consideration was given to allow her to be buried in Arlington National Cemetery, but upon her request she was buried with full military honors in the Fort Bragg cemetery in North Carolina, as an honorary colonel in the U.S. Marines and an honorary lieutenant colonel in the U.S. Army.

Who was this incredibly unselfish woman, born as Margy Reed? It was none other than Martha Raye, one of America's most loved entertainers. Martha has two stars on the Hollywood Walk of Fame, one for motion pictures and one for television, but the brightest star will forever shine as the U.S. military's unselfish and devoted warrior who loved the troops and never failed them. Thank you, Martha!

Play Ball!

CARL HAD NO children of his own but he loved spending time with his young nephews, especially playing baseball. The problem seemed to be that there was no place to play other than backyards and alleyways. The year was 1938 and Carl made a decision to create an organized program for his nephews and other local children so their summers could be filled with the joy of baseball.

Carl gathered a few of the neighborhood children, enlisted the help of his brothers George and Bert, as well as their wives, to assist with his dream of an organized program. No official games were played that lazy summer, nor did they have a name for their "unofficial league." In 1939 that all changed.

Carl, George, and Bert started three teams with sponsors. Lycoming Dairy, Lundy Lumber and Jumbo Pretzel supported each of the teams and the three brothers acted as managers of each team. Locals John and Peggy Lindermuth soon joined the group and formed the Board of Directors. After talking with friends in the community Carl came up with a name for the organization, "Little League." His idea was to provide a wholesome program for the boys in Williamsport, Pennsylvania.

The three original sponsors paid $30 each to keep the cost to parents at a minimum and limited the rosters to 30 boys on each team. On June 6, 1939, the first Little League game was played. Lundy Lumber defeated Lycoming Dairy 23-8. Lycoming came back to win the seasons first half title and ended up with a rematch against Lundy

Lumber for the summer championship in a best of three series, which Lycoming Dairy won with a final game victory of 3-2.

From these humble beginnings Little League Baseball has become the world's largest organized youth program from those original three teams to over 200,000 teams in all 50 states and more than 80 countries. The goals of the organization have never changed, to give young people of the world a game that provides the fundamental principles of sportsmanship, fair play and teamwork.

The story of Little League Baseball is a lesson for all of us. If you have a dream and a burning passion to make a difference, if your idea benefits others and you are willing to think beyond the stars, you can change the world. If you get some time this summer, leave work a little early, pick up some popcorn and a soda, and enjoy an afternoon watching young boys and girls living the dream. I think you will feel young again! Maybe, just maybe, you will find someone with whom you can play catch. Life is good when there is baseball!

Put Me in Coach!

IT IS ONE of those lazy summer days, warm breeze, white clouds, the smell of freshly cut grass, and softball. It is just a softball camp, but a little different than most. You see, all the players were different but in the same way. They are all missing something, yet they also have so much more than the average person.

The 20 kids in the camp are often made fun of at school, so the camp becomes a special place where they are not only treated with respect, but expected to perform to their full potential. They go far beyond expectations with the incredible circumstances they have to overcome. 10-year-old Adrian Grejeda is one of those extraordinary kids. He can run, jump, hit, and field ground balls better than before—the "before" being an incident that occurred in his young life. You see Adrian is like every kid at the camp, they are all amputees. Some are missing an arm, others a foot or an entire leg. Many had developmental problems from birth while others like Adrian were accident victims. "It's cool because you don't feel alone," he said. "And they can teach you stuff that you don't know."

There is no time for self-pity here and no one is given any special treatment because of a handicap. How could they with the coaches that work the camp? You see, they are amputees also, all wounded warriors who lost limbs while in the service of America. They have a special connection with these positive and energetic kids and in most cases learn more than the young athletes about courage and the passion to succeed.

Susan Rodio started the camp in Orlando, Florida. After volunteering with the Wounded Warrior Softball Team, she saw what an impact the players were having on children with amputations who were assisting the team as batboys and batgirls. She wanted to create a camp where that impact could go even further. Now twenty kids are selected each year and they are coached exclusively by the members of the Wounded Warriors Softball Team.

On the last day of camp, the children get to put their new skills to the test on a real minor league field. They get to stand at home plate and run the bases usually reserved for the pros. After the game, 9-year-old Jen Castro said she would have great stories for her friends when she got home.

"I learned how to do everything better," she said. "I learned how to have courage in life and not to just give up on anything."

Justin Feagin, who lost his leg in 2010 to an IED in Afghanistan, said he hoped he and the other wounded warriors left the children with a few simple words to remember.

"Our team motto is 'Life without a limb is limitless,' and so I hope they take that back with them," he said. Twenty kids living a dream, but more than that twenty kids and a group of wounded veterans end the camp with healed hearts, renewed courage and a new outlook on life. There is no greater handicap than a handicap of the mind. Physical handicaps are merely challenges to reach new levels of achievement and greatness!

The Import

LIKE MOST OTHER countries, Japan was hit badly by the Great Depression of the 1930s. In 1938, Soichiro Honda was still in school when he started a little workshop, developing the concept of the piston ring. His plan was to sell the idea to Toyota. He labored night and day, even slept in the workshop, always believing he could perfect his design and produce a worthy product. He was married by now, and pawned his wife's jewelry for working capital.

Finally, he completed his piston ring and was able to take a working sample to Toyota, only to be told that the rings did not meet their standards! Soichiro went back to school and suffered ridicule when the engineers laughed at his design.

He refused to give up. Rather than focus on his failure, he continued working towards his goal. Then, after two more years of struggle and redesign, he won a contract with Toyota.

By now, the Japanese government was gearing up for war! With the contract in hand, Soichiro Honda needed to build a factory to supply Toyota, but building materials were in short supply. Still he would not quit! He invented a new concrete-making process that enabled him to build the factory. With the factory now built, he was ready for production, but the factory was bombed twice and steel became unavailable, too. Was this the end of the road for Honda? No! He started collecting surplus gasoline cans discarded by US fighters. "Gifts from President Truman," he called them, which became the new raw materials for his rebuilt manufacturing process. Finally, an earthquake destroyed the factory.

After the war, an extreme gasoline shortage forced people to walk or use bicycles. Honda built a tiny engine and attached it to his bicycle. His neighbors wanted one, and although he tried, materials could not be found and he was unable to supply the demand. Was he ready to give up now? No!

Soichiro Honda wrote to 18,000 bicycles shop owners and, in an inspiring letter, asked them to help him revitalize Japan. 5,000 responded and advanced him what little money they could to build his tiny bicycle engines. Unfortunately, the first models were too bulky to work well, so he continued to develop and adapt, until finally, the small engine 'The Super Cub' became a reality and was a success. With success in Japan, Honda began exporting his bicycle engines to Europe and America.

End of story? No! In the 1970s there was another gas shortage, this time in America and automotive fashion turned to small cars. Honda was quick to pick up on the trend. Experts now in small engine design, the company started making tiny cars, smaller than anyone had seen before, and rode another wave of success.

Today, Honda Corporation employs over 100,000 people in the USA and Japan, and is one of the world's largest automobile companies. Honda succeeded because one man made a truly committed decision, acted upon it, and made adjustments on a continuous basis. Failure was simply not considered a possibility.

Truly inspiring, isn't it? Another stalwart who has overcome all odds to make Honda a household name with sheer dedication and hard work.

The Unlikely Sharpshooter

KAROLY TAKACS. YOU'VE probably never heard of him. However, in Hungary, he's a national hero. Everyone there knows his name and his incredible story. After reading his story, you'll never forget him...

In 1938, Karoly Takacs of the Hungarian Army, was the top pistol shooter in the world. He was expected to win the gold in the 1940 Olympic Games scheduled for Tokyo. Those expectations vanished one terrible day just months before the Olympics. While training with his army squad, a hand grenade exploded in Takacs' right hand, and Takacs' shooting hand was blown off.

Takacs spent a month in the hospital depressed at both the loss of his hand, and the end to his Olympic dream. At that point, most people would have quit and spent the rest of their lives feeling sorry for themselves. Most people would have quit, but not Takacs. Takacs was a winner. Winners know that they can't let circumstances keep them down. They understand that life is hard and that they can't let life beat them down. Winners know in their heart that quitting is not an option.

Karoly decided he would continue to pursue his Olympic dream and in 1948 he set his target on the London Olympics. Just to make the team would have been a feat of heroic proportions, to be in the top ten would have been achieving the impossible, but to win? No one expected him to even be in contention ... but win he did. It would be one thing if it were rifle shooting, but this was different, it was competition in pistol shooting. It was hard enough to be the best with an athlete's normal shooting hand, but to totally relearn the event with the opposite hand was unheard of in shooting. There was one person who believed it could be done and on that warm summer afternoon in London, England in 1948, Karoly Takas won the Olympic Gold Medal in shooting.

Belief, passion, endless hours of hard work and taking action are a formula for miracles every time. You can feel sorry for yourself about current circumstances or you can rise above the crowd and climb upon the victory stand of life. What's your choice? After all it is merely a choice.

Gone Fishin'

THE YEAR WAS 1971 and young Johnny was frustrated. No matter where he looked he could not find the lures and equipment he needed for his passion, fishing. Finally out of frustration he rented a U-haul trailer and traveled across the southeastern United States collecting the best fishing tackle he could find. When he returned home he set up and 8' X 8' space in his father's liquor store. They were located in an area that was popular with sports fisherman and the word got out quickly that Johnny was the man with the right equipment.

When the anglers returned home he started getting calls to mail his wide range of products all over the U.S. The demand was so great that in 1974 he created his first catalog and began mailing it to hundreds of customers across America. In 1978 he introduced his first professionally rigged boat, motor, and trailer "fish ready package."

By now you might have guessed the name of the company that started in a small corner of a liquor store as Bass Pro Shops, now expanded into every area of outdoor sports and living. Each store is unique and delivers a fascinating experience with the typical customer staying for several hours. They have over 70 stores and are the world's largest online and catalog retailer of outdoor equipment.

With no money, no real plan, no experience starting or running a business, Johnny Morris beat the odds. Sometimes not knowing the obstacles, not understanding why you "can't do something" and believing with all your heart you will succeed beats the experts and the "know it all's."

What is the lesson? One person on a mission of excellence and determination defeats all odds. What are the odds that Johnny Morris could have grown an 8 X 8 space into stores of over 300,000 square feet and become the largest retailer of outdoor equipment in the world? Apparently the odds are pretty good! If you haven't visited one of these stores you are in for a pleasant surprise and an adventure. Go, Johnny, Go!

The Race of a Lifetime

GAIL DEVERS WAS a child prodigy. Growing up she was always the fastest runner in school and as a senior in high school won both the 100-meter dash and 100-meter hurdles. She had her pick of colleges based on her incredible talent and work ethic and chose UCLA. She continued to improve and it became obvious to her coaches that she was going to be a world caliber athlete. By her senior year in 1988, Devers was ranked one of the top female hurdlers in the country. That year, she set a national record in the 100-meter hurdles with a time of 12.61 seconds and qualified to compete for a spot on the 1988 U.S. Olympic Team.

She participated in the 1988 Olympic Games in Seoul, Korea but her performance was well below expectations. She began to feel fatigued and experienced muscle pulls and cramps. Her event performance was slower than she had run in high school. Her condition continued to worsen and included impaired vision, migraine headaches, convulsions, and extreme weight loss. A UCLA team physician she encountered by chance noted that Devers' eyes were bulging and she had a goiter on her throat, both symptoms of a thyroid condition. Tests confirmed that Devers had Graves' disease, an autoimmune disorder resulting from an overactive thyroid gland, and that the growth on the gland would have soon become cancerous. Devers underwent radiation treatment to destroy the growth, but the treatment also destroyed her thyroid gland. She had to start taking a synthetic thyroid medication, something she would most likely be forced to do for the rest of her life.

She refused to give up her dream of world and Olympic greatness and continued her track training, but 1991 however was not an easy year. The radiation treatment alleviated many of Devers' symptoms and she resumed her training. Complications began to surface however, including the formation of blood blisters on the soles of her feet and between her toes. Walking became so painful that Devers often had to crawl or be carried, and one doctor discussed amputating her feet. Once the radiation treatments were stopped her symptoms disappeared. Through hard work and perseverance she performed better than ever and qualified for both the World Games and the 1992 Olympics.

The following summer, Devers placed second in the 100-meter hurdles at the World Championships in Tokyo, Japan, set a new U.S. record in the event at a meet in Berlin, Germany, and qualified for the 1992 Olympics in Barcelona, Spain, in both the 100- meter dash and the 100- meter hurdles. Devers stunned spectators when she won the 100- meter dash, beating second place finisher, Julie Cuthbert of Jamaica, by .01 seconds and logging her personal best time in the event. She hit the last hurdle in the 100-meter hurdles and finished fifth.

The Gail Devers story is one of hope and perseverance. We all face tragedies and failures in our lives, often not of our own making. We can drown ourselves in sympathy or we can bathe ourselves in determination and belief that the only real failure is in not trying. Gail Devers now spends her time helping others who are at a disadvantage in life, inspiring them to dream and to fight for their dreams as she did in her incredible comeback effort.

By the way, 1992 was not the end of the Gail Devers story. In 1996, she became the second woman in Olympic history to win the 100-meter dash in two consecutive games, and she brought home a second gold medal for her performance in the 4x100 relay. She competed in the 100- meter hurdles as well, but placed fourth.

The great Winston Churchill said, "Continuous effort—not strength or intelligence—is the key to unlocking our potential." There are no barriers that cannot be overcome, no rivers that cannot be crossed, no mountains that cannot be climbed by those who refuse to quit.

Thoughts to Live by

WOULD YOU LIKE your life to be filled with a little more joy, humility, integrity, and love? Here are a few things to practice daily. If we all did these, life would change for the better very quickly!

Treat your spouse or significant other as if it were always the first date.

If you can count your close friends on two hands, you are a fool. If you can count them on one hand, you are truly blessed.

When disciplining your children, subordinate, or co-worker, always do it with a mixture of quiet resolve and sincere caring. Anything else is casting stones.

Never take yourself too seriously. After all, you are human, which means you will never get it right. So learn to laugh at your mistakes.

Little things mean a lot. The quiet touch, the kind word, the undeserved compliment, a simple smile, the thank you note, the kind voicemail will never fail to touch someone's heart and just maybe change them for the better. Very few do the little things consistently… be one of them.

Anger and hate toward someone else is like taking poison and waiting for the other person to die. They seldom spend much time in worry or stress while you are shortening your life.

The law of cause and effect applies to human emotion. What you give out is what you will get in return. Give out negativity and you will get the same. Give out enthusiasm and positive emotions and it will come back to you tenfold.

Do what you say you are going to do, do it when you say you are going to do it, and do it the way you said you would do it… you will be respected, honored, and always in demand.

Save your best for those whom are closest to you. If you come to your loved ones with leftover energy and emotion, they will feel like "leftovers." Save your best for those who count most.

Always be kind to the young, patient with your peers, and honorable toward the old, at some time in life you will have been all three.

Take this final thought; live each day as it were your last. Fill it with hope, kindness, passion, and dreams, and the results will be amazing. You will never be short on laughter, joy, and friends!

In a Pickel!

HIS FIRST FOOD company went bankrupt in 1875 and he was barely able to feed his own family. Banks, without a Federal Reserve to provide stability, called in their loans. He was arrested twice for an inability to return borrowed money. Although he wasn't jailed, he was humiliated when the news hit the front page. His parents were also hit, pledging their brickyard to help and losing it to his creditors.

He bounced back with a vengeance in 1876, launching his firm with brother John and cousin Frederick. His reputation for quality and integrity helped his rebuilding, which let him repay his creditors by 1879.

By 1880, annual sales reached $198,000—worth $4.5 million now and the rest is history. Who was this young businessman? Henry J. Heinz. Even at a young age he showed an aptitude toward innovation and possessed a relentless work ethic. By the age of 9 years old he was selling vegetables door to door along with his own brand of horseradish! At the age of ten years old he worked in his father's brickyard. In just a few short years he was a master bricklayer, had his own four-acre garden by the age of twelve and used the profits to buy a horse and carriage to deliver to local merchants.

By age twenty-four he owned his own brickyard and the following year, he and a friend formed Heinz, Noble & Co. to market bottled condiments and pickled food, in high demand by Americans tired of their bland diet.

Heinz quickly realized he could position his products to charge a premium by using the best ingredients and putting them in clear glass jars; competitors used dark ones to conceal their use of cheaper filler material that ranged from turnips to sawdust.

"Heinz positioned his product line, factories, and sales organization to capitalize on the rise of the new grocery chains like A&P in the late 19th century," said Michael Mullen, senior vice president for corporate and government affairs at H.J. Heinz. "He once said, 'A real leader does not wait for opportunity, but makes one himself.' He also applied the latest technology to production lines to process food faster and in larger quantities, eventually operating them around the clock."

In addition to maximizing the distribution benefits provided by railroads, Heinz visited trade exhibitions and factories across America and in Europe and embraced new technology.

A turning point in his company's marketing came in 1893 at the Columbian Exposition in Chicago.

"Heinz's booth was on the second floor in a remote location that made it easy for fairgoers to ignore," wrote Larry Schweikart and Lynne Doti in "American Entrepreneur." "He quickly assessed the problem and had a printer make small white cards that offered a free pickle to anyone presenting the card at the booth. It attracted such large crowds that fair officials had to strengthen the supports of the gallery floor. By the time the fair had ended, Heinz had given away one million pickles, and newspapers and magazines publicized the stunt nationally."

CPSIA information can be obtained at www.ICGtesting.com
Printed in the USA
LVOW10s1153020116

468693LV00003B/7/P